Twelve English Statesmen

CHATHAM

CHATHAM

BY

FREDERIC HARRISON

London

MACMILLAN AND CO., Limited

NEW YORK: THE MACMILLAN COMPANY

1905

CONTENTS

CHAPTER I

CHAPTER I

INTRODUCTORY

Posterity, this is an impartial picture. I am neither dazzled by the blaze of the times in which I have lived, nor, if there are spots in the sun, do I deny that I see them. It is a man I am describing, and one, whose greatness will bear to have his blemishes fairly delivered to you—not from a love of censure in me, but of truth; and because it is history I am writing, not romance.

SUCH was the judgment passed on Chatham by a hostile contemporary, whose *Memoirs* were withheld from the public eye for nearly a century after their compilation. In these words Horace Walpole sums up his incisive character of "the terrible cornet of horse" whom Sir Robert Walpole attempted to muzzle, of the aspiring orator who contributed so much to the fall of Sir Robert, of the imperious statesman who finally succeeded to more than the power of Walpole at his zenith, reversed his policy, and entirely recast the international position of Great Britain in the world.

In eight centuries our country has known but four great creative statesmen: men who, to use the words of a well-known historian, have been "founders or creators of a new order of things." William the

A

Conqueror made all England an organic nation. Edward the First conceived and founded Great Britain. Cromwell made the United Kingdom and founded our Sea Power. Chatham made the Colonial System and was the founder of the Empire. For good and for evil, through heroism and through spoliation, with all its vast and far-reaching consequences, industrial, economic, social, and moral—the foundation of the Empire was the work of Chatham. He changed the course of England's history—nay, the course of modern history. For a century and a half the development of our country has grown upon the imperial lines of Chatham's ideals; and succeeding statesmen have based the key-note of their policy on enlarging the range of these ideals, in warding off the dangers they involved, in curbing or in stimulating the excesses they bred.

Frederick of Prussia said of Chatham, "England has long been in labour, and has suffered much to produce Mr. Pitt: but at last she has brought forth a man." By France, the rise and fall of Chatham was watched as equivalent to the loss or the gain of a decisive campaign. His hyperbolic self-will, his almost grotesque arrogance, seemed excused by the deference of all with whom he acted, and the timidity of all whom he confronted. Contemporary memoirs ring with anecdotes of his personal ascendency and the terror he inspired at home and abroad. When Chatham said to a colleague, "I know that I can save this country, and that no one else can," it was not regarded as arrogance and presumption, but was treated as simple truth, which no doubt it was. Walpole's famous character of Chatham, from which a sentence heads this chapter, runs thus : " The admirers of Mr. Pitt extol the reverberation he gives to our councils, the despondence he banished, the spirit he infused, the conquests he made, the security he affixed to our trade and plantations, the humiliations of France, the glory of Britain carried under his ministrations to a pitch at which it never had arrived—and all this is exactly true."

In his own age and in ours, Chatham has cast a spell over men's minds, and has usually been spoken of in superlatives of praise and of blame. In Westminster Abbey we read, that it was during his administration that Great Britain was exalted "to a height of prosperity and glory unknown to any former age." In the Guildhall we read that William Pitt was raised up by Providence "as the principal instrument in His memorable work." Both these public monuments were erected many years after the statesman's fall and retirement. The first was ordered by Parliament under the ministry of Lord North, whom Chatham so fiercely opposed and denounced. The second inscription was composed by Edmund Burke, his opponent and severe judge. The French Abbé Raynal, in his History of Indian Commerce (of 1780), declared that Chatham "raised the heart of England so high, that his administration was nothing but a chain of . conquests." Lord Brougham, in his *Historical Sketches*, tells us that Chatham "is the person to whom every one would point if desired to name the most successful statesman and the most brilliant orator that this country ever produced." Lord Macaulay, in many things his severest critic, in his fine description of the monument in the Abbey, concludes that "history, while for the warning of vehement, high, and daring natures, she notes his many errors, will yet deliberately pronounce, that, among the eminent men whose bones lie near his, scarcely one has left a more stainless, and none a more splendid name." In our own time Mr. J. R. Green is fascinated by "the personal and solitary grandeur" of Chatham, "by the depth of his conviction, his passionate love of all he deemed lofty and true, his fiery energy, his poetic imaginativeness," "his purely public spirit." "He loved England with an intense and personal love. He believed in her power, her glory, her public virtue, till England learned to believe in herself." Mr. Lecky has said : "With all his faults he was a very great man—far surpassing both in mental and moral altitude the other politicians of his generation." As Lord Shelburne, the colleague and successor of Chatham, records that he was a man "of a most extraordinary imagination," so the descendant and historian of Shelburne speaks of the great orator "as the eternal monument of the highest eloquence employed on the noblest objects."

The reverberation of these achievements has passed away. The long and crowded epoch of Chatham's son tended to make men forgetful of the father, who far outlived the span of his own power; and the tremendous events that followed the French Revolution and the Empire of Napoleon overshadowed the reign of George II. But history will continue to dwell with praise or with blame, with sympathy or with sorrow, on the lonely chief who breathed a new soul into his countrymen, who planted the saplings which have grown into a mighty forest, who inspired that passion for transoceanic expansion which has led to such energies, such miseries, such glory, and such heart-burning.

There seem to be peculiar difficulties in attempting to write the life of a statesman whose work so many of our statesmen have sought to imitate, whose methods and doctrines so many others have condemned. Chatham is usually regarded as pre-eminently a "war minister." And undoubtedly he "organised victory" on a scale greater than that achieved by any other English statesman. Though he never saw a battle-field in his life, he is reported to have said that "he loved honourable war." If he loved war for itself, as Alexander and Napoleon did, it is an indelible blot upon his name. The great-grandson of Chatham's colleague and successor, speaking before Chatham's monument in the Guildhall of London, has in our generation denounced "the scourge and calamity of a needless war." But it must not be forgotten that Chatham's wars were singularly sparing of blood, suffering, and ruin, to the victors as to the conquered. They have resulted in permanent conquests and settlements unexampled in modern history. The memory of these results has too often obscured the magnificent and far-seeing efforts of Chatham towards international justice, domestic reform, and peaceful progress. In many of the aims of good government he anticipated the work of his successors. In ages to come, this perhaps will be his true glory. Mr. Lecky has said: "No minister had a greater power of making a sluggish people brave, or a slavish people free or a disaffected people loyal." Of how many of our statesmen could this noble eulogy be passed? But, as Walpole reminds us, such a man must be painted as he was, with all his faults and all his failures. The glamour of his personality is nothing to us now. We have "to write history, not romance."

CHAPTER II

WILLIAM PITT was born on the 15th of November 1708, of an honourable and wealthy family, settled in the West of England. Until he entered Parliament at the age of twenty-six, nothing but a few bare facts have been recorded of his life; nor have eulogists or critics given us a very definite picture of his boyhood and youth. It seems as if the majestic personality, which so deeply overawed his contemporaries, had caused his biographers to abstain from searching into the story of their hero's life, until he had become a striking character in the political world. "Of his infancy and early youth I have not been able to collect any authenticated information," sighs the most obsequious of his biographers. For biographical purposes, "The Great Commoner" had no youth. The bare facts extant are soon told.

William was the younger son of Robert Pitt, M.P. for Old Sarum, who was the eldest son of Thomas Pitt, of Swallowfield, Berks, and of Boconnoc in Cornwall, who was also M.P. for Old Sarum, his own borough. In the genealogy prefixed to the authorised *Life*, the Pitt family is traced back to Nicholas Pitt,

7

temp. Henry VII. (or Henry VI.), through a John Pitt, clerk of the Exchequer, *temp.* Elizabeth, a Thomas Pitt, seated at Blandford, Dorset, and another John Pitt, rector of Blandford, who was great-grandfather of the statesman. Lord Shelburne, who was himself a Fitzmaurice, in his autobiography says that Pitt was a younger son "of no great family." Lord Chesterfield called it a "very new family." But in the fulsome biography compiled by the Rev. Francis Thackeray—an uncle, by the way, of our great satirist —the "respectability" of the Pitt family is vouched by the intermarriages of that house with men and women of rank and condition. The historian, whom his nephew might have classed as a "clerical snob," is indignant that the Earl of Chatham should be called a *novus homo.* He gives us a Sir William Pitt, 1636, ancestor of Lord Rivers, two Thomas Pitts, father and son, and a Ridgeway Pitt, all three Earls of Londonderry, uncle and cousins of the statesman. He records also another uncle, John Pitt, as marrying the sister of Viscount Fauconberg, and an aunt, Lucy, who married James, first Earl Stanhope. "Be this as it may"—to use the formula of genealogists—it is clear that the Pitts were a race which, not being of the highest influence or descent, had been allied during some generations with families of rank and name.

The most conspicuous of Chatham's ancestors was his grandfather, Thomas Pitt, who in an adventurous life of seventy-three years (1653-1726) amassed fortune and reputation abroad. There are so many traits of likeness between this bold adventurer and his grandson, that the study of atavism demands a few words on his career. Thomas Pitt as a youth engaged himself first as a sailor, and then in a miscellaneous trade in India, settled in Bengal, and for twenty years carried on a battle with the East India Company as an "interloper" on their monopoly. On one occasion he was bound over not to engage in illicit business in £40,000, on another he was fined £1000. He remained impenitent, irrepressible, and triumphant. Having brought the Company to terms, he was for twelve years Governor of Madras, which he successfully defended against the Nawab of the Carnatic.[1] He purchased estates in England, and was elected to the Parliaments of 1689, 1690, and 1695. From 1710 till 1715 he represented Old Sarum. He was appointed Governor of Jamaica, but he did not go out to the island. "He always knew what to do, and he did it." He was a man of indomitable energy and infinite resource, by which he amassed considerable fortune, which he invested in English estates.

Governor Pitt married Jane Innes, who, we are told, traced descent from James Stewart, Earl of Moray, natural son of James v. of Scotland; and

[1] During his stay at Madras he kept up a constant search for large diamonds, from which he obtained the name of "Diamond Pitt." His great *coup* was the purchase of the historic Pitt diamond, which he acquired in 1701 for £20,400. He sold it in 1717 to the Regent of France for £135,000. It weighed, before cutting, 410 carats, and it now weighs 136 carats. It is the second diamond in the world, and is still preserved in the State Jewels of France in the grand Apollo Gallery of the Louvre. It was recently valued at £480,000. Under the Empire, it was set in the hilt of Napoleon's sword of ceremony. Thus, by one of the ironies of history, the stone which bought a seat in Parliament for Chatham adorned "the sword of Austerlitz," which broke the heart of Chatham's son.

patriotic Scots have made much of this legendary descent. Having amassed great fortune—and no doubt other speculations of his besides the diamond returned him seven hundred per cent. on his outlay— he settled in the West of England, and purchased from the widow of Lord Mohun, the famous duellist, the fine estate of Boconnoc in Cornwall. It lay on a tributary of the Fowey, four miles east of Lostwithiel, near the scene of the Royalist victory of Bradock Down in 1643. Boconnoc—which is said to have the finest grounds in the county—is, however, but incidentally connected with Chatham. He was certainly not born there, as used to be said, for he was ten years old when his grandfather purchased the estate. Governor Pitt, who died in 1726, before Chatham was eighteen, devised Boconnoc to Robert Pitt, his eldest son, who died in the following year; and then the estate descended to Thomas, the statesman's elder brother. It passed ultimately through the Grenvilles by marriage to the Fortescue family, who scrupulously preserve the Chatham memorials and portraits that remain there.

It would appear from the Fortescue Papers (*Hist. MSS. Com.*) that the Governor himself was something of a rough diamond. His spelling is original, and his style abrupt. And his family seems to have been both quarrelsome and thriftless. Robert Pitt, the father of the statesman, the eldest of three sons of Governor Pitt, married Harriet Villiers, daughter of the fifth Viscount Grandison, of Ireland. They had two sons, of whom the statesman was the younger, and five daughters. Three of these daughters married gentlemen of good estate, and one of them became Maid of Honour to Queen Caroline. The critical Lord Shelburne declared that they were profligate and mad. Thomas, the elder brother of Chatham, married the sister of the first Lord Lyttelton, of Hagley in Worcestershire, and became the father of the first Lord Camelford. Chatham himself, as we shall see, married the sister of Richard Grenville, the first Earl Temple. This sketch will show us at once the family connections between the houses of Pitt, Villiers, Stanhope, Temple, Grenville, and Lyttelton.

It is certain from the books of Trinity College, Oxford, that Chatham was born in the Parish of St. James, Westminster. Along with Chaucer, Bacon, Milton, Pope, and Byron, he serves to refute Carlyle's empirical law that "it is impossible but that a London-born man should not be a stunted one." Of the boyhood of Chatham almost nothing is recorded, except "a family tradition" which we fain would accept on the authority of an eminent relative. The first Earl Stanhope, general and statesman, who in courage, energy, and sagacity, bore some resemblance to Chatham, noticed the genius of the boy, his nephew by marriage, and would call him "the young Marshal." The "young Marshal" was sent to Eton at an early age, was on the foundation, and had for schoolfellows the first Lord Lyttelton, Henry Fox, the first Lord Holland, Henry Fielding, author of *Tom Jones*, and Charles Pratt, Lord Chancellor Camden. Lord Shelburne, his colleague, relates that Chatham was "distinguished at Eton," but that he took an unfavourable view of the school system. One of his sayings was: "He scarce observed a boy who was not cowed for life at Eton—a public school might suit a boy of a turbulent forward disposition"—a temperament which Chatham was not himself conscious that he possessed. But he certainly was not "cowed for life at Eton." From Eton he went to Trinity College, Oxford, where he entered as a gentleman-commoner in January 1727, when he was just eighteen. He was subject to gout even as a boy; and he suffered from it so severely whilst at Oxford that he left the University, and was advised to travel. He did not take a degree, and spent some time in France and Italy. But he could not shake off the disease. During life he remained a martyr to it, and we shall see how cruelly the affliction reacted upon his whole nature and his public career.

Feeble health, we are told, made young Pitt a reader, and he gave himself to history and the classics. The Latin verses he published at Oxford on the death of George I. in 1727, if we allow for a few solecisms or misprints, are not below the standard of such college exercises. Lord Stanhope tells us that the favourite authors of the young orator were Thucydides, Demosthenes, and, in English, Bolingbroke and Barrow. He would translate the classics into fluent English prose; he read and re-read Barrow's sermons, till he could repeat them by heart. He was also a constant reader of Spenser's *Faëry Queen*. And he would read Shakespeare aloud to his family. Chatham never was a scholar in the strict sense: like most great orators, he was rather a poor writer, too often stilted and usually bald. Nor is there any evidence that he possessed any serious learning or natural gift for literature. But it is plain that his powerful mind had assimilated such history and poetry as was most akin to his nature. As Lord Stanhope tells us, he was early "warmed by the flame" of the records of the past and by the great books of the ancient and the modern world.

Chatham's letters show us that he was full of the familiar classics, which he quotes continually and aptly. His letters to his nephew, the first Lord Camelford, give us the picture of a noble mind well read in the best authors. He assists him in translating Virgil's *Eclogues* into verse. He insists on his reading the *Aeneid* "from beginning to ending." He hopes that he loves the *Iliad* and the *Aeneid*: they contain "lessons of honour, courage, disinterestedness, love of truth, command of temper, gentleness of behaviour, humanity, and in one word, virtue in its true signification." He recommends Locke, Burnet, Bolingbroke, Lord Clarendon's *History*, May on the Parliament. Lord Granville, editing these letters, very aptly quotes Milton:—"I call that a complete and generous education which fits a man to perform justly, skilfully, and magnanimously, all the offices both public and private, of peace and war." That complete and generous education Chatham had.

After his father's death, the elder brother having succeeded to the family estates, William Pitt embraced the profession of arms, and at the age of twenty-three he obtained a commission as Cornet in the Blues, apparently by the interest of its colonel, Lord Cobham, whose niece was the wife of his brother Thomas. Lord Chesterfield tells us that the income of the young soldier at this time was but £100 a year. Of his military career, which lasted only four years, we know nothing, nor need we indulge the speculations of his reverend panegyrist and his martial uncle that he would have gained glory as a great commander.

He applied himself to the art of war with characteristic ardour, for he told Lord Shelburne that, as Cornet, there was not a military book he had not read through. If he had any such dreams himself, they were cut short in an unexpected and quite dramatic way. On February 7, 1735, William Pitt was returned as member of Parliament for Old Sarum, the proverbial "rotten borough," which had been bought by Diamond Pitt, and had been represented by him and by Robert Pitt, his son. William entered the House of Commons in the later years of Walpole's long administration, a time when a vehement and determined opposition was led by William Pulteney, whose party were known as the "Patriots."

The reign of Sir Robert Walpole was now being slowly undermined, though his consummate skill as a tactician still maintained a dull, venal, fickle majority. His insatiable grasp of power had driven from his side all men of ability and force. The sinister genius of Bolingbroke scattered on all sides the seeds of discontent. Wyndham led the opposition in a tone of fierce denunciation. Townshend, Pulteney, Chesterfield, Carteret had left the veteran. His sagacious scheme of Excise had aroused such indignation in the nation that it was withdrawn to avoid an outbreak;

but the Duke of Bolton and Lord Cobham, who opposed it, were cashiered and deprived of their regiments by a scandalous abuse of ministerial pressure. The great minister's most successful policy—peace abroad and quiet business at home—had enriched the nation by leaps and bounds, whilst it irritated the King, alarmed the patriots, and met ceaseless ridicule from the public and the press. The Prince of Wales, the unlucky "Fred" of the *Memoirs*, naturally became the centre of opposition to his father and his father's counsellor. Round him gathered the leaders of the Opposition, claiming to be the true "Old Whigs of the Revolution," whose historic policy it was to curb the power of the Crown. Swift, Pope, Gay, Thomson, and Arbuthnot supplied the malcontents with brilliancy and satire; and both within and without the Parliament, spasmodic attempts were continually hatched to bring about a coalition with the Jacobite factions. In face of all these opponents, Sir Robert still contrived to maintain his sinking authority by a marvellous union of courage, energy, sagacity, and tact.

It was the hour for the rise of a great orator, and the greatest orator who has ever trod the floors of Parliament had now appeared on the stage. When Sir Richard Temple, of Stowe, had succeeded to a splendid estate and great influence by his family connections, he revived the title of Lord Cobham. His sister Hester married Richard Grenville, and his sister Christian married Sir Thomas Lyttelton. Thomas Pitt, the elder brother, married a daughter of Sir Thomas, a sister of George, the first Lord Lyttelton, whilst

William Pitt, the Chatham that was to be, married the second Hester, the daughter of Richard Grenville, the sister of George, the first Earl Temple. This was the famous cousinhood of the "Boy Patriots," who now formed a brilliant clique in society and in Parliament. Leicester House, the abode of the Prince of Wales, was their Court. Their rendezvous in the country was the royal domain of Stowe, whose master was the uncle of George Grenville and of George Lyttelton, and whose two nieces married the two Pitts.

William Pitt, Cornet in the King's own horse, entering the House of Commons as member for the family borough of Old Sarum, did not immediately show his powers. It was not till 29th April 1736 that he made his maiden speech, when he supported Pulteney's motion for an address of congratulation to the King on the marriage of Frederick, Prince of Wales. The speech has been reported with absurd encomiums by his flatterers, and is denounced as "empty and wordy" by Macaulay. Empty and wordy it is, if we look on it as the conventional compliments on a royal marriage. If we consider the circumstances and the persons, it was a political attack of curious insolence. The marriage had been forced on the Prince by the King. Congratulations were moved, not by the King's friends, but by the bitter opponent of the dominant minister. It was supported with fulsome exaggerations by the avowed partisans of the Prince, a son who hated his father, and whom both his parents detested. To rise up and talk, as young Pitt did, of the King's "tender, paternal delight in indulging" his odious heir, of "the humble request of his submissive and obedient son," when that son was meditating rebellion and the father was meditating how to disinherit the traitor—this was not the language of official compliment. And if we imagine this fierce irony rehearsed with all the sonorous dignity and the dramatic emphasis which gave such thrilling power to Chatham's eloquence, we can easily understand the effect it produced.

At any rate the great minister took it as a formidable challenge. We know from his biographer that the debate "gave great offence and tended still further to widen the breach"—between Prince's friends and King's friends, between the minister and his opponents. The "warm panegyric bestowed on the Prince," "the cold praises given to the King"—say rather, the outrageous laudation of a mischievous fool, and the savage irony poured on a jealous monarch—struck home. Walpole, they tell us, declared, "We must muzzle this terrible Cornet of horse." Pitt was at once cashiered and his commission cancelled. Within a few weeks, "the supersession of Cornet Pitt" was recorded and filled up, as that of Lord Cobham had been cancelled three years before for opposing the Excise. Walpole had already tried seduction; for Pitt himself told Lord Shelburne that Sir Robert "had offered him the troop which was afterwards given to General Conway." As promises and rewards had not availed, the great corrupter now tried penalties.

Sir Robert's cynical worldly wisdom did not quite measure the heroic temper of the tiro. He did not muzzle the terrible young cornet. He merely whetted his taste for blood.

B

The soldier who thus had bounded into the front rank of parliamentary forces was now in his twenty-eighth year. Nature had given him every physical advantage. He was tall, with an elegant and commanding figure. Grace and dignity marked every gesture and attitude. It is clear that Chatham from youth had studied to improve his natural gifts. Writing to his nephew at Cambridge, being himself a bachelor in middle life, he says, "Behaviour is of infinite advantage or prejudice to a man." "Behaviour is certainly founded in considerable virtues." "As to the carriage of your person, be particularly careful, as you are tall and thin, not to get a habit of stooping." Politeness, he says, is "benevolence in trifles or the preference of others to ourselves in little, daily, hourly occurrences in the commerce of life." "To inferiors, gentleness, condescension, and affability, is the only dignity." Good servants are "*humiles Amici*, fellow Christians, *Conservi.*"

We have ample records of the orator's person. The head was small and the countenance thin; the nose was aquiline and long; the eye "that of a hawk." All the descriptions record the wonderful power of that eye, in language which would be treated as extravagant were it not that its effect is vouched by so many competent witnesses. A Catholic lawyer who had seen Pitt thus describes him in that oft-cited passage: "In his look and gesture grace and dignity were combined, but dignity presided; the 'terrors of his beak, the lightning of his eye,' were insufferable. His voice was both full and clear; his lowest whisper was distinctly heard, his middle tones were sweet, rich,

and beautifully varied ; when he elevated his voice to
its highest pitch, the House was completely filled with
the volume of the sound. The effect was awful, except
when he wished to cheer and animate ; he then had
spirit-stirring notes, which were perfectly irresistible.
He frequently rose, on a sudden, from a very low to a
very high key, but it seemed to be without effort.
His diction was remarkably simple, but words were
never chosen with more care "—" the terrible was his
peculiar power. Then the whole House sank before
him,—still, he was dignified ; and wonderful as was
his eloquence, it was attended with this most important effect, *that it impressed every hearer with a conviction that there was something in him even finer than his
words ; that the man was infinitely greater than the orator."*

That is the peculiar keynote of Chatham's power
of speech. It had great defects. He was called a
tragedian, and no doubt he was a consummate actor.
A wit declared that he was "the Cicero and the
Roscius of his age in one." His enemy, Horace Walpole,
said that he was equal to Garrick. Macaulay says
that "on the stage he would have been the finest
Brutus or Coriolanus ever seen." He knew the in-
stantaneous effect upon such an audience of real
dramatic passion. And Chatham let his passion boil
over. He was no subtle debater, artful to follow out
an argument in all its reasoning and refute it step by
step. But he would crush an opponent with a fierce
retort, a burning sarcasm, or a thrilling appeal. His
style was at times florid, forced, hyperbolic : but even
then it was no piece of studied rhetoric ; it was the
turgid inspiration of the moment. It has been well

said : " He was the slave of his own speech "—"no English orator was ever so much feared."

Of the effect of his oratory we have unimpeachable evidence. Walpole tells how " he crushed" Lyttelton, "crucified" Murray, "lashed" Granville, "punished" Newcastle, "attacked" Fox. Lord Chesterfield, a keen and sardonic judge, relates that "his invectives were terrible, and uttered with such energy of diction, and such dignity of action and countenance, that he intimidated those who were the most willing and the best able to encounter him. Their arms fell out of their hands, and they shrunk under the ascendant which his genius gained over theirs." Lord Walde-grave said, " He has an eye as significant as his words." Wilkes, whom Chatham despised and rebuffed, wrote of him : " He was born an orator, and from nature possessed every outward requisite to bespeak respect, and even awe. A manly figure, with the eagle eye of the famous Condé, fixed your attention, and almost commanded reverence the moment he appeared, and the keen lightning of his eye spoke the high respect of his soul, before his lips had pronounced a syllable. There was a kind of fascination in his look when he eyed any one askance. Nothing could withstand the force of that contagion. The fluent Murray has faltered, and even Fox shrank back appalled from an adversary ' fraught with fire unquenchable,' if I may borrow the expression of our great Milton."

As hardly a single adequate specimen of Chatham's oratory has been fully reported, and even as we read the bald reports that survive, we have no means of calling up the tones, the gestures, and the look which

filled them with living fire, we must accept the con-
current witness of those who heard him, as to the
direct power of his words.   Mr. Goldwin Smith has
finely said, "only a few flakes of his fiery oratory
remain."   The *Memoirs* abound in stories of the abject
silence in which the House would submit to Pitt's
mandates, in anecdotes of his opponents cowering
under his invectives.   We who read the speeches of a
public man by our fireside, or catch some distant
echoes of his voice in a crowded hall, are ready to
smile at the tale of members of Parliament cowering
before a minister, as if they were boys in the lower
school before the inexorable Dr. Keate.   But we may
remember that in the first half of the eighteenth
century the House of Commons was a close corporation of gentlemen who were believed to be still under
the spell of noble deportment and full of respect for
the lofty bearing of the *vieille cour* of Kensington and
Versailles.

   An age which values itself on being nothing if not
practical, commonplace, free-and-easy, and sceptical, is
wont to sneer at the value of eloquence, and to despise
it as a literary artifice.   But eloquence is of two kinds.
There is the verbose advocacy of Cicero before the
Praetor ; there is the heroic appeal of Demosthenes to
his fellow-citizens.   The first is literature ; the second
is statesmanship.   How does a statesman achieve his
ends, unless it be by using words which convince
others and fill them with his own convictions and
spirit ?   Speeches may be rhetorical displays ; they
may also be the trumpet of battle, the springs of
action the determining cause of great policies and far-

reaching deeds. The speeches of Mirabeau, Danton, of Washington, of Patrick Henry, or Charles Fox, were not rhetorical exercises; they were strokes of state-craft and calls to action. So in the main were those of Chatham.

All contemporary evidence bears out the decisive judgment of Charles Butler that, quite apart from his eloquence, there was in the speeches of Chatham that which made men feel there was "something in him finer than his words; that the man was infinitely greater than the orator." It was not so much the rhetoric, it was not even the intellect, which conquered and dominated his hearers. It was the moral power, the man himself. Frederick of Prussia said, "England has brought forth a *man*." The Duke of Cumberland, the King's brother, said "that is a man." "His great-ness will bear to have his blemishes fairly delivered," said Horace Walpole. He was, said the critical Lord Chesterfield, "what the world calls 'a great man.'" Of no orator in ancient or in modern times have we more definite testimony of the direct power of his personality over those who heard him. In the words of a contemporary : "Those who have been witnesses to the wonders of his eloquence—who have listened to the music of his voice, or trembled at its majesty— who have seen the persuasive gracefulness of his action, or have felt its force; those who have caught the flame of eloquence from his eye—who have rejoiced at the glories of his countenance, or shrunk from his frowns,—will remember the resistless power with which he impressed conviction."

Of modern historians Carlyle, with all the hyper-bolic fanaticism of his creed, has best expressed this sense of power in the man, of the conviction impressed by his words on those who heard him speak. Pitt's speeches, he writes, "are not Parliamentary Eloquences, but things which with his whole soul he means, and is intent to *do*." "Pitt, though nobly eloquent, is a Man of Action, not of Speech; an authentically Royal kind of Man. And if there were a Plutarch in these times, with a good deal of leisure on his hands, he might run a Parallel between Friedrich and Chatham. Two radiant Kings; very shining men of Action both." Pitt's speeches, the historian of Frederick concludes, "are full of genius in the vocal kind, far beyond any Speeches delivered in Parliament: serious always, and the very truth, such as he has it; but going into many dialects and modes; full of airy flashings, twinkles and coruscations. A singularly radiant man."

Many years had to pass before the orator became master of the State. But, from the first, Pitt's speeches in Parliament were rather actions than orations. It was not parliamentary eloquence, such as was that of his son, of his son's rivals, of Fox, or Sheridan, or Burke. From the first, the words of William Pitt were the strokes of a man of action, of the fighting man, of the leader of men, of the states-man. We need no longer regret that the words have not been recorded. It was the man, not his words, which mastered the nation. The genius of the man was expressed in acts, in results, which reacted upon Europe, on the East and the West. It is the career of the statesman, not of the orator, that we have now to follow. It is Pitt, the creator of the Empire: Chatham, the one man who might have saved it from humiliation and disruption.

CHAPTER III

THE RISING ORATOR

THE young orator, who had won the ear of the House of Commons and incurred the ill-will of King and Ministers by his maiden speech, steadily advanced in reputation both in Parliament and in the press. His dismissal from the Cornetcy gained him fresh favour from the Prince of Wales and from Lord Cobham, and it caused excitement amongst officers of the army, who saw how deep official resentment could descend. Early in the following year, 1737, Pulteney, the Opposition leader, moved for the settlement of £100,000 a year on the Prince, a project which Walpole and George resisted almost as if it were an act of treason. Again Pitt supported the motion with all his force in a speech which was said to be masterly, and which certainly caused intense irritation in the Court. The organ of the Government attacked him "as a young man of overbearing disposition," and with coarse jibes told him that, though his neck was long and his body lean, he must not therefore fancy himself a "new Tully." Thereupon the Opposition organ compared him to Demosthenes in his youth. Lyttelton in clumsy verse hailed his friend as destined to "lead the

24

patriot band." The poet Thomson hymned praises to the "pathetic eloquence" that moulds "the attentive Senate" and "shakes Corruption on her venal throne." Another bard found in him "a Roman's virtue with a courtier's ease." Lord Cobham told a friend that in a short quarter of an hour Pitt "can persuade any man of anything." After a fierce debate, the settlement on the Prince was lost by a small majority. The King drove his son from St. James's Palace. The Prince retaliated by making Pitt groom of the bed-chamber, and Pitt's cousin, Lyttelton, his private secretary.

The question which raised Pitt from the level of a brilliant orator to that of a political power was the great issue which absorbed the whole of his career and justifies his claim to creative statesmanship. It was at bottom the formation of a transatlantic dominion: the problem as to whether the North American seaboard and commerce should be under British or Spanish and French control. The international questions were complex and inveterate, the rights were disputed, and the facts were uncertain. Nor is this the place to unravel that tangled business. By ancient treaties, confirmed at the Peace of Utrecht in 1713, the trade of England and of Spain with the Atlantic colonies was limited and regulated. Spain possessed vast territories in Central America, together with the West Indies, and Florida. She asserted a strict monopoly of commerce with her own colonies, to be secured by the right of search and of seizing contraband goods even on the high seas. She had cross-claims against the South Sea Company for the supply of negro slaves to her colonies, and had conceded to

Englishmen the privilege of sending one ship yearly to trade in her ports.

All through Walpole's time the trade of England had been growing by leaps and bounds. She had thriven under a policy of peace, whilst the European powers were intriguing and fighting. Along with trade, her settlements in America had been greatly enlarged. And ever since the victory of La Hogue in 1692, when the French fleet had been annihilated, she had made good her predominance at sea. In spite of treaties, an immense illicit trade with the Spanish colonies had been developed. Contraband had become a system. The *one* ship was simply the blind for a whole fleet of attendant merchantmen. For a time it suited the Spanish Government to submit to the British system of smuggling; but at last very violent and savage reprisals were made by the Spanish coast-guard. These again were bitterly resented and grossly exaggerated, so that the whole country, the City and exchanges, the navy, the press, and Parliament were filled with incessant stories of outrages, insults and spoliations, of which some were fictions, some were exaggeration, and some were undoubtedly true. True or false, the nation from end to end was quivering with wrath and humiliation. The American historian of Sea-Power has said : " Walpole was now face to face with one of those irrepressible conflicts between nations and races to which compromise and repression can only be employed for a short time. War arose out of the uncontrollable impulse of the English people to extend their trade and colonial interests."

There were causes much deeper and more solid.

When at last the union of France and Spain under
Bourbon princes had become a working reality—that
union against which William III. and Marlborough had
fought so long—a secret treaty was made between
France and Spain, the Family Compact of 1733, an
essential aim of which was an alliance of the two
powers to destroy the maritime ascendency of England,
and to cripple her transmarine possessions. The
treaty itself was not known, but its effects were soon
seen, and its existence was suspected. A long series
of disputes between England and Spain gathered up :
—outrages on British merchants, the boundaries of
Florida with Georgia and Carolina, the debts of the
South Sea Company, Gibraltar, Minorca, and cross-
claims of many kinds. The right of search is always
odious, and a source of irritation when temporarily
exercised in war. A permanent right of search apart
from a state of war, rigorously exercised against peaceful commerce on the high seas, could not long be
endured by a great trading nation, especially by a
nation which claimed to be predominant at sea. It
was idle to appeal to the clauses of treaties twenty-
five years old, which had long been suffered to lie
dormant. The King, the merchants, the people, the
seamen, were all eager to end the quarrel by war.

Walpole, still resolute to maintain his policy of
peace and industrial development, resisted the clamour
with his usual energy and skill. Deserted or betrayed
by his own colleagues, and deprived of the help of the
Queen, he still kept his majority in Parliament, whilst
he met the storm of opposition by masterly sagacity,
firmness, and diplomatic genius, till, in spite of his own

judgment, and by a gross sacrifice of principle, he was at last forced into declaring war with Spain himself. There can be no doubt that, under the letter of treaties, the gravamen of the Spanish claim, the right in peace to search merchant ships on the high seas and confiscate their cargo at will, was technically to be justified. In truth, it cannot now be doubted that, on a balance of Spanish illegalities with British, the burden lay on our country. Nor was it long concealed that much of the outcry was extravagant and artificial. But a question far wider and deeper lay behind. The real issue was this. Was England to have the predominant share in settling the American continent and in developing the trade of the New World ?

It is plain that the war with Spain could not be justified on moral grounds, hardly by any view of international law. But we can now see that it was inevitable, and we can fairly decide what have been the practical results of the war of 1739 and of the succeeding wars of George II.'s reign. The conquest of England by William I., the conquest of Wales by Edward I., the trial and execution of Charles I., and the Revolution of 1689, like the seizure of Silesia by Frederick II., had great and permanent results, but they cannot be judged by abstract or legal tests. Had Walpole's policy of peace and industry succeeded in stifling the indignation of the nation, had it been consistently carried out by him and by his successors during the reign of the Georges, the nineteenth century would certainly have found the larger part of the transatlantic colonies French and Spanish : the dominion and trade of the seas not very unequally shared by the great European powers : and England conceivably in the position of a greater Holland. Some believe that this result would not have been injurious to the progress of general civilisation. There can be no doubt whose brain and will it was that contrived and effected a very different issue.

As a device for calming the growing irritation at home, Walpole made a convention with Spain whereby the questions at issue as to trade, as to the limits of Florida and Carolina, and the minor issues, should be settled by a Conference ; that Spain would pay an indemnity of £95,000, and even this sum was reduced by a Spanish counter-claim at the last moment to £27,000. The announcement of this Convention roused a perfect fury in the nation. They had to pay a heavy sum for what the public had regarded as a glorious victory ; the claims to indemnity for outrage and spoliation, trifling as they were, had to be set off against the debts of a trading company on the slave traffic ; the limits of Georgia were left undefined ; above all, the right of search was entirely omitted, for the finesse of Walpole had made the fatal blunder of dropping out of sight the real issue at stake.

It was on the 8th of March 1739 that the House of Commons met for the grand attack on this feeble expedient to delay the inevitable war. Such was the excitement that 400 members took their seats at eight o'clock in the morning. The Minister's brother moved a somewhat fulsome address of congratulation on "the final determination" of the disputed claims, on obtaining "speedy payment" for losses, with reliance that the King would protect his subjects from

search on the open seas, and would settle the limits of
his American dominions. This was what the nation
demanded, but the Convention did nothing of the
kind. Amidst the torrents of indignant eloquence
poured out by the Opposition, that of Pitt is the most
famous. The substance is this :—

"We have here the soft name of a humble address to the
Throne, and for no other end than to lead to an approbation
of the Convention. Is this cursory disquisition of matter of
such variety and extent all we owe to ourselves and to our
country? *When trade is at stake, it is your last entrenchment;
you must defend it or perish.* . . . Here we are taking sanctuary
in the Royal name, instead of meeting openly and standing
fairly the direct judgment and sentence of Parliament upon
the several articles of this Convention.

"You are moved to vote a humble address of thanks to his
Majesty for a measure which is odious throughout the kingdom. They try a little to defend it on its own merits; if
that is not tenable, they throw out general terrors—the House
of Bourbon is united, who knows the consequence of a war?
Sir, Spain knows the consequence of a war in America; whoever gains, it must prove fatal to her; she knows it and must
avoid it; but she knows that England dares not make it. If
this union be formidable, are we to delay only till it becomes
more formidable, by being carried further into execution and
by being more strongly cemented? But be what it will, is this
any longer a nation? Is this any longer an English Parliament, if, with more ships in your harbours than in all the
navies of Europe, with above two millions of people in your
American colonies, you will bear to hear of *the expediency of
receiving from Spain an insecure, unsatisfactory, dishonourable
Convention?* It carries fallacy or downright subjection in
almost every line.

"As to the great national objection, Sir, the searching of
your ships, it stands merely in the preamble of the Convention,
but it stands there as the reproach of the whole, as the
strongest evidence of the fatal submission that follows. On
the part of Spain, an usurpation, an inhuman tyranny, claimed

and exercised over the American seas. On the part of England, that which is an undoubted right by treaties, and from God and nature declared and asserted in Parliament, is referred to plenipotentiaries to be discussed, limited, and sacrificed.

"The Court of Spain has plainly told you that you shall navigate by a fixed line to and from your plantation and in America; if you draw near to her coast (and this is an unavoidable necessity) you shall be seized and confiscated. If upon these terms only she has consented to refer disputes, what becomes of the security which we are flattered to expect? I will take the words of Sir William Temple:—*It is vain to negotiate and to make treaties if there is not dignity and vigour enough to enforce their observance.* Under the misconstruction of these very treaties, this intolerable grievance has arisen. It has been growing upon you, treaty after treaty, through twenty years of negotiation. Spain seems to say, We will treat with you, but we will search and take your ships; we will sign a Convention, but we will keep your subjects prisoners in Old Spain; the West Indies are remote; Europe shall witness in what manner we use you.

"The right claimed by Spain to search our ships is one thing, and the excesses admitted to have been committed under this pretended right, is another. Giving an indemnity for excesses is no cession of the claim to search. The payment of the sum stipulated (seven and twenty thousand pounds, and that, too, subject to a drawback) is evidently a fallacious nominal payment only. I will not attempt to enter into the detail of a dark, confused, and scarcely intelligible account. Can any verbal distinctions, any evasions whatever, explain away this public infamy? To whom would we disguise it? To ourselves and to the nation? I wish we could hide it from the eyes of every court in Europe. They see that Spain has talked to you in the language of a master.

"This Convention, Sir, I hold from my soul to be nothing but a stipulation for national ignominy; an illusory expedient, to baffle the resentment of the nation. A truce without a suspension of hostilities on the part of Spain, but with a real suspension on the part of England. As to Georgia, it is a suspension of the first law of nature, self-preservation and self-defence. It is a surrender of the rights and trade of

England to the mercy of plenipotentiaries. The complaints of your despairing merchants and the voice of England have condemned it. Be the guilt of it upon the head of the adviser. God forbid that this House should share the guilt by approving it."

These thunderous invectives, the essential points in which were real and true, shook the House and excited the nation. The Minister fought on with his back to the wall; his skill and his prestige secured him still a narrow majority. But within a few months he was driven into a war reluctantly undertaken and feebly conducted. We may wonder to-day that a statesman of the experience and sagacity of Walpole should imagine that diplomatic verbiage could stem the torrent of such passion and such pride. Sound sense, consummate adroitness, elaborate dispatches, are not the last words in the ruling of states : nor are peace and plenty the sole life-blood in the organism of nations.

The war was ill-managed, and the Opposition called for an inquiry into the orders given to the Admiral. Pitt again thundered in support of this investigation (October 1740) :—

"Our time cannot be more usefully employed, during a war, than in examining how it has been conducted, and settling the degrees of confidence that may be reposed in those to whose care are entrusted our reputations, our fortunes, and our lives.

"There is not any inquiry, Sir, of more importance than this ; it is not a question about an uncertain privilege, or a law which, if found inconvenient, may hereafter be repealed. We are now to examine whether it is probable that we shall preserve our commerce and our independence, or whether we are sinking into subjection to a foreign power.

"But this inquiry, Sir, will produce no great information, if those whose conduct is examined are allowed to select the evidence; for what accounts will they exhibit but such as have often already been laid before us, and such as they now offer without concern? Accounts, obscure and fallacious, imperfect and confused; from which nothing can be learned, and which can never entitle the Minister to praise, though they may screen him from punishment."

Such was the language used by the "Great Commoner" to a government which was seeking to hoodwink the nation and to burke inquiry. Such was the responsibility of ministers in a war as understood by one who was soon to "organise victory" himself. William Pitt was certainly not too ready to be satisfied with the assurances "of the right honourable gentleman," nor was he in the least afraid of being accused of want of patriotism, if he presumed to attack the government during the course of a war.

At this time, it must be admitted, Pitt allowed himself a violence, we may even say a fury, which would shock our more decorous days. In 1741, a Bill was brought in "for the encouragement and increase of seamen, and for the better and speedier manning of his Majesty's fleet." In fact, it authorised search-warrants to arrest seamen even in private houses, by day or by night, and to press them into the service. Although Pitt was a warm friend of the navy and a supporter of the war, he could not stand this. He said:—

"Will this increase your number of seamen? or will it make those you have more willing to serve you? Can you expect that any man will make himself a slave if he can avoid it? Can you expect that any man will breed up his child to be a slave? Can you expect that seamen will venture their lives or their limbs for a country that has made them slaves? or can you expect that any seaman will stay in the country, if he can by any means make his escape? If you pass this law, Sir, you must do with your seamen as they do with their galley-slaves in France—You must chain them to their ships, or chain them in couples when they are ashore. . . . For God's sake, Sir, let us not put our seamen into such a condition as must make them worse than the cowardly slaves of France or Spain.

"I say, and I do not exaggerate, we are laying a trap for the lives of all the men of spirit in the nation. Would any of you, Gentlemen, allow this law to be executed in its full extent? If, at midnight, a petty constable with a press-gang should come thundering at the gates of your house in the country and should tell you he had a warrant to search your house for seamen, would you, at that time of night, allow your gates to be opened? I protest, I would not. Would any of you patiently submit to such an indignity? Would you not fire upon him, if he attempted to break open your gates? I declare I would, let the consequences be never so fatal; and if you happened to be in the bad graces of a Minister, the consequence would be, your being either killed in the fray, or hanged for killing the constable or some of his gang."

This specimen may serve to show the passion that Pitt imparted into debate. He was no braggart, nor was he thought to be mouthing. He always spoke without preparation, and gave full rein to the tempest of his feeling at the moment. At the time, he no doubt fully believed himself willing to shoot the constable and defend the sanctuary of his home. And we may note how his eloquence boiled over with interrogations. From the days of the Philippics and *Quousque tandem, Catilina?* impassioned oratory has ever rested more in questions than in bald asseveration.

Other well-known examples of the sharpness of Pitt's tongue may be mentioned here. When Walpole's brother taunted the orator with his youth (by the way, he was thirty-two), the terrible cornet replied—or Dr. Johnson put in his mouth, the famous retort :—

"The atrocious crime of being a young man, which the honourable gentleman has with such spirit and decency charged upon me, I shall neither attempt to palliate nor deny, but content myself with wishing that I may be one of those whose follies may cease with their youth, and not of that number who are ignorant in spite of experience."

The rest is surely rank Johnsonese, as when he went on :—

"The wretch who, after having seen the consequences of a thousand errors, continues still to blunder, and whose age has only added obstinacy to stupidity, is the object of abhorrence or contempt, and deserves not that his grey head should secure him from insults.

"Much more is he to be abhorred, who, as he has advanced in age, has receded from virtue, and becomes more wicked with less temptation ; who prostitutes himself for money which he cannot enjoy, and spends the remains of his life in the ruin of his country."

Alas! Sir Robert Walpole did not succeed in muzzling the terrible cornet. And this is how he met the charge of his theatrical gestures :—

"If any man shall, by charging me with theatrical behaviour, imply that I utter any sentiments but my own, I shall treat him as a calumniator and a villain ; nor shall any protection shelter him from the treatment which he deserves. I shall on such an occasion, without scruple, trample upon all those forms with which wealth and dignity entrench themselves, nor shall anything but age restrain my resentment ; age, which always brings one privilege, that of being insolent and supercilious without punishment.

"The heat that offended them is the ardour of conviction, and that zeal for the service of my country, which neither hope nor fear shall influence me to suppress. I will not sit unconcerned while our liberty is invaded, nor look in silence upon public robbery. I will, at whatever hazard, repel the aggressor, and drag the thief to justice, whoever may protect them in their villainy, and whoever may partake of their plunder. And if the honourable gentleman——"

Here the orator was interrupted by a call to order, but he seems to have silenced and overwhelmed his accuser.

It is impossible to say how much of this was really spoken by Pitt. We may take it that, if most of the rhetoric was Johnson's, all the passion was Pitt's. It is plain that the Parliament of the Walpoles, of the Pelhams, and the Pulteneys was not very tolerant of oily evasions, that fine art of modern ministers ; and it was perfectly familiar with downright accusation and gross personalities.

The ill success of the war with Spain increased the irritation against Walpole, and in February 1740 an address was moved to request the King to dismiss his minister for ever. The excitement was great. The passages and galleries of the House were thronged. Five hundred members attended, many of them at six o'clock in the morning. Pitt took an active part in the great debate. Unfortunately, his speech has been reported in sententious and stilted Johnsonese, which can give no true idea of what he said. That its substance was a searching denunciation of Walpole's ministry, and its form a fierce philippic of impetuous indignation, is clear enough.

Pitt said the Treaty of Hanover was now discovered to be for the advancement only of the House of Bourbon—our armies were kept up only to multiply dependence and to awe the nation—Spain had been courted only to the ruin of our trade—the Convention had been an artifice to amuse the people—the Minister had alienated us from the Empire, our only friend, and thus had endangered the liberties of Europe. Why was the Plate fleet spared? Why were our ships sacrificed to the worms? Why were our sailors poisoned in an unhealthy climate? Why do the Spaniards laugh at our armaments and triumph in our calamities? The lives of Hosier and his forces are charged against this man. They were murdered to pacify the British and to gratify the French.

A minister who betrays an army to defeat, who impoverishes a nation, who compels our armies to perish without a blow in sight of our enemies—a minister who has doomed thousands to the grave, who has co-operated with foreign powers against his country, who has protected its enemies and dishonoured its arms—such an one should lose not only his honours, but his life; at least he should be stripped of those riches he has amassed during a long career of successful wickedness; he should be stopped from increasing his wealth by multiplying his crimes.

"But, Sir, no such penalties are now required. We do not recommend an Act of Attainder or a Bill of Pains and Penalties. We ask only that he be removed from that trust which he has so long abused."

Here at last we can hear the roar of Pitt's wrath in the solemn apophthegms of the pseudo-Johnson. All this was, no doubt, outrageous violence, but it was not empty rhetoric. At the time, Pitt believed all this, and all the hot spirits in the nation felt the same. Walpole's majority carried him through this onslaught.

But in a few months he was forced to appeal to the nation. The issue went against him. On 2nd February 1742 he quitted the House of Commons. On the 11th, as Earl of Orford, he resigned office for ever.

During the election of 1741 Pitt had been again returned for Old Sarum He took a dark view of the state of the country. In a private letter to Lord Chesterfield he said : "I think the scene abroad a most gloomy one. Whether day is ever to break forth again, or destruction and darkness is finally to cover all—*impiaque æternam meruerunt sæcula noctem*—must soon be determined." "France by her influence and her arms means to undo England and all Europe." Pitt was perfectly sincere even in his most violent moods. And in his most private hours he was ever meditating heroics in what our critic used to call "the grand manner." It was the man's inborn temperament.

Walpole's resignation by no means abated the rancour with which he was pursued, and no one was more bitter than Pitt, who hotly supported the motion for a secret inquiry into the acts of the late administration during the last twenty years. They are pleased to call it rhetoric, he said, but a man who speaks from his heart in the cause of his country naturally uses vehement expression. When there is a general clamour without doors, an inquiry is the only means of satisfying the public. We are not pressing for an impeachment on specific charges. We insist on an inquiry in order to see what specific charges have to be made. The people will become disaffected to their Sovereign if they find him obstinately employing a minister who oppresses them at home and betrays them abroad.

They confess that our affairs both at home and abroad
are at present in the utmost distress. But, say they,
you must free yourselves from this distress before you
inquire into the causes of it. *If so, a minister who has
plundered and betrayed his country, has nothing to do but
to involve it in a dangerous war or some other great distress,
in order to prevent an inquiry into his conduct,* just as a
thief, after plundering a house, sets it on fire that he
may escape in the confusion. For twenty years we
have been under one man, and now find ourselves on
a precipice. He is no longer at the Treasury, but he
is not removed from Court, nor will his influence be
withdrawn until he is sent to the Tower.

In the same strain of violence Pitt denounced the
government measures as to the South Sea Company, as
to public credit, as to the Civil List, as to the abortive
Excise scheme, as to the Sinking Fund, as to the Salt
duty, and as to "the weakness and wickedness" of
many other measures of "our late (I fear I must call
him our present) Prime Minister." When he turned
to foreign affairs, Pitt was even more violent. He
said the Treaty of Hanover was the source of the
danger to which Europe is exposed, for assenting to
which ministers must have had some secret, perhaps
some corrupt, motive. They excuse themselves for
shrinking from war with Spain. But *we were* at war.
Spain was carrying on war with our trade during the
whole of their negotiations. Spain knew that nothing
could provoke that minister to go to war, or, if anything did, it would be conducted in a weak and miserable manner. He behaved as if the House of Austria
were our real enemy. Our warlike preparations were

a mere electioneering device; they were not intended to overawe Spain or France. And then "the infamous convention with Spain," which sacrificed our trade and free navigation, abandoned Georgia, and reduced the indemnity of £500,000 or £600,000 to a paltry £27,000. We acquired nothing; we gave up everything.

"By these weak, pusillanimous, and wicked measures we are become the ridicule of every court in Europe, and have lost the confidence of all our ancient allies." "We are upon a dangerous precipice, and we cannot get off it, whilst our councils are influenced by the late Minister who still has access to the King's closet. His punishment, be it ever so severe, will be but a small atonement of the past. His impunity will be the source of many future miseries to Europe as well as to his country. Let us not sacrifice our liberties to the preservation of one guilty man."

This thunderous philippic so nearly succeeded that, in a division of 486, Walpole only escaped by two votes. He was in imminent danger of impeachment. But his consummate skill in tactics, his prestige and sagacity, the confidence of the King, and divisions amongst his enemies, saved him from trial, and he gradually regained much of his influence and fame. A second attempt to obtain an inquiry was made shortly afterwards; and Pitt again was in the front of the attack. He began by repeating many of the same arguments for investigation, but he added some outrageous suspicions floating about, as that Walpole had given Spain and France secret information. What is very remarkable in Pitt's attitude was this—that he insisted on the existence of public rumour and popular indignation as an all-sufficient ground for parliamentary inquiry. "The general voice of the

people of England ought always to be a sufficient
ground." Here was the germ of one of the new
ideas which Pitt was to infuse into political life.
"The ill posture of our affairs both abroad and
at home; the melancholy situation we are in; the
distresses to which we are now reduced, are sufficient
cause for an inquiry. The nation lies bleeding, perhaps expiring. The balance of power has been fatally
reduced." There was a suspicion too that public
money had been applied to corrupt influence in elections. Had not posts, pensions, and preferments been
the bribes offered for votes in Parliament? Had not
officers in the army been promoted or cashiered
according as they supported or opposed any measure
of the Court? Whilst a commission remains at the
absolute will of the Crown, the officers of our army
will be the slaves of a minister, and will help him to
make slaves of us all. The orator wound up with
fierce insinuations about misapplication of the civil
list in bribing the electors, about the need of a
general account of past treasury payments, how the
steward of the nation had built sumptuous palaces
whilst living beyond his visible income, and amassing
great riches. And when young Horace Walpole spoke
in defence of his father, Pitt cried out, "He does well
as the child of his father, but we are the children of
our country!"

In a house of 497, the secret Committee was carried
by a majority of seven. Pitt himself served on it;
but nothing resulted from its proceedings. And the
iniquitous attempt to obtain witnesses by offering
them an indemnity was properly extinguished in the

House of Lords. Such is a sketch of Pitt's first
great political achievement—securing the fall of
Walpole. Furious as was his attack, and savage as
were the suspicions he chose to make himself responsible for in Parliament, there was no personal malignity
in his accusations. He believed them to be well-
founded: a majority of politicians in the country
believed them to be well-founded. Some of the
charges certainly were well-founded. However high
we may rank the peace policy of Walpole's long
administration of twenty years, however great his
services to the growth of prosperity, order, and
stability in the kingdom, it cannot be denied that
much of his influence had been cynical and grossly
corrupt. It was impossible to govern a nation which
was boiling with irritation, and had just grounds of
irritation. And at last Walpole committed the un-
pardonable crime of entering into a war which he
regarded as a wanton and useless aggression; and,
what was even worse, remaining to carry it on with
half a heart and culpable indifference.

Pitt had acted with unreasoning passion in a kind
of patriotic delirium; but his pleasant altercation
across the floor of the House, first with the elder, and
then with the younger Horace Walpole, seemed to
show that he was not actuated by personal malice.
The story that he was a party to an underhand
intrigue to screen Walpole upon certain terms has
been too hastily accepted by Macaulay, who found it
in a later edition of Coxe's *Memoirs*. A vague bit of
backstairs gossip repeated five years after date by a
quarrelsome fribble like Frederick, Prince of Wales,

to a loose-tongued scandalmonger like the poet Glover, is not sufficient guarantee for a story as utterly inconsistent with the character of Pitt as it is with the circumstances of Walpole. To me, the tale is as unintelligible as it is worthless.

Pitt lived to regret some of the violent things he had said, and was quite as bitter towards Walpole's successors as he had been towards Walpole himself. And the large-hearted and sagacious Orford lived long enough to recommend Pitt to Henry Pelham for office in his ministry. He wrote to the Prime Minister just forming his new government—"Pitt is thought able and formidable; try him or show him." Pitt had to wait twelve years more before he was even tried. But in the eighteenth century the only administrations which stand forth in the history of England after that of Walpole, are those of Pitt and then of Pitt's son.

CHAPTER IV

THE ASPIRANT FOR OFFICE

THE four years that elapsed from the retirement of
Walpole until Pitt at last, in his fortieth year, forced
himself into a minor office, were years of incessant
intrigue and change, both at home and abroad, of
European wars, coalitions, and compacts, of dissolving
parties, alliances, and administrations.   Pitt all this
time fought desperately for his own hand.   He was
in the zenith of his powers, acknowledged as the
greatest orator in Parliament, conscious, perhaps too
conscious, of his genius, with a great reputation in the
country, but with office closed to him by the rooted
antipathy of the King and his own subordinate place
in that intensely oligarchic world.   Power was the
monopoly of a set of great and wealthy nobles, who
had their own clans, their nominees in the Commons,
and their protectors in the Royal Family, itself divided
into different branches and cliques.   The only one
of the great peers who stood by Pitt was the famous
Earl of Chesterfield, in some ways the finest intellect
of them all, but a peer who acted apart and controlled
no such powerful combinations as did the Russells, the
Pelhams, the Cavendishes, and the Grenvilles.   It was

44

a cruel chance that this able and honest man was permanently debarred from office by incurable deafness. The rest feared Pitt more than they desired his alliance. His proud independence and his passionate self-assertion were qualities ill-fitted to succeed in that babel of small intrigue, and insidious fawning on the Court and the magnates.

It would serve no purpose to rehearse all the kaleidoscopic changes in the politics and the ministries of the time. And he would be a daring friend to Pitt who attempted to justify all the shifts and inconsistencies of his restless activity. As Macaulay showed, the gushing Thackeray only made himself ridiculous when he painted his hero as "a finished example of moral excellence." Pitt could not be right, as his eulogist pretends, both when he sought to send Walpole to the Tower and also when he extolled him, when he denounced the Spanish right of search in opposition and when he submitted to it as minister, when he attacked Newcastle and when he joined him, when he thundered against subsidies, and when he lavished them on foreign allies beyond all other ministers.

Pitt's career, especially at this time, was full of incongruities. He was above all things an *opportunist*, as we say to-day ; and in times of change a real statesman must be opportunist, as were Cromwell, William of Orange, Henry IV., and Richelieu. Walpole's fall was in part due to his obstinate consistency in grasping sole power for twenty years, in governing by corruption and intrigue, and in staving off war at any sacrifice. In an age of change and confusion, consistency may become a grave political fault. It is a fault with which Chatham certainly cannot be charged. He was a man of passionate impulses, sudden to condemn, arrogant, proud of his own virtue and patriotism. Conscious of his own high aims and his great superiority to the men around him, whose jealousies and intrigues were crushing him, Pitt made not a few blunders, some of which he had the grace to acknowledge in his later and cooler moods. But with all his outbursts, we may almost say his incoherences, with his fierce ambition, which in so great a man was almost a virtue, Pitt remains a man of honour, a patriot of a grand nature, who towers above his rivals in an age of sycophancy, corruption, and treachery, as much in his stormy faults as he does in his heroic ideals.

Walpole's retirement from office, but not from influence, did not mean any great change in policy, and not very much in men. The brilliant Carteret, the vacillating Pulteney, the tricky Newcastle, the learned Hardwicke, the corrupt Henry Fox, could not control the great party which had been formed by the energy and sagacity of Walpole. Chesterfield and Pitt were both excluded from the new administration; and Pitt was as loud as ever in opposition. For a time Carteret was the leading minister, engaging in European wars and entanglements with reckless unwisdom. When he proposed to Parliament to take 16,000 Hanoverian troops, Pitt broke out. Far from attempting to conciliate the King, he sought to wound him in his most sensitive place.

"Why should we squander public money, he asked, on armies which are only intended to make a show to our friends whilst they are a scorn to our enemies? These Hanoverians marched into the Low Countries as a place of security, to be farthest from the reach of their enemies. In the next campaign we shall be asked to hire Hanoverians to eat and sleep. They tell us that we are bound by England's signature to the Pragmatic Sanction to defend the Queen of Hungary. But the Elector of Hanover was equally one of the parties to that treaty. Why does he not send his own troops to defend the Queen? And why should we pay his troops for doing that which Hanover is bound to do? This great, this mighty nation, Sir, is considered only as a province to a despicable Electorate. These troops are hired only to drain us of our money. Every year shows this absurd, ungrateful, and perfidious partiality towards the German interest, yearly visits to that *delightful* country, sums spent to aggrandise and enrich it. Let us perform our duty as representatives of the people: and if ministers prefer the interests of Hanover, Parliament regards only the interests of Great Britain."

On the fulsome address to the King on his return after the battle of Dettingen, December 1743, Pitt again thundered against the Hanoverian policy of war in defence of the Empress-Queen.

"From one extreme our administration have run to the very verge of another. Our former minister [Walpole] betrayed the interests of his country by his cowardice; our present minister [Carteret] would sacrifice them to his quixotism. Our former minister was for negotiating with all the world; our present minister is for fighting with all the world. Our former minister was for agreeing to every treaty, however dishonourable; our present minister will give ear to none, although the most reasonable that can be desired. Both are extravagant. The only difference is that the wild system of the one must subject the nation to much heavier expenditure than ever did the pusillanimity of the other."

The inconsistency of this from one who became the greatest of war ministers is more apparent than real. Pitt's interest from the first was, and remained through life, in the transoceanic empire of Britain, and not in European complications. To him the wars and combinations between the states of Central Europe—wars and combinations so dear to the German heart of George II. and to the vapouring ambition of Carteret—were sheer waste of English strength and wealth. Pitt's ideals were based on British commerce, navigation, sea-power. India, the Atlantic provinces from Cape Breton to Florida, the West Indies, were the aim of his schemes and hopes. For them he would fight and tax his people. To waste them and their resources on the Elbe, the Rhine, and the Danube he ever regarded as a criminal folly. France and Spain, from whom he wrested their Indian and Atlantic supremacy, were the true enemies. Prussia, Austria, or Italy did not concern us. And from the point of view of the founder of our transmarine empire Pitt was undoubtedly right.

Pitt went on to complain that we had not pressed the Queen of Hungary to come to terms with Frederick of Prussia when he seized Silesia. He complained of our joining the coalition against Frederick. It was done in the interest of Hanover. What should have been done was to bring about a reconciliation between the Princes of Germany, in order to establish a new balance of power. We ought to have embraced the

opportunity of peace and have insisted on it, instead
of urging the Queen to resist Prussia and France,
when we might have arranged things on the terms of
Uti possidetis.

He then fiercely attacked the conduct of the war,
going so far as to say that the ardour of the British
troops had been restrained by the cowardice of the
Hanoverians, that we had left to the enemy after our
fortunate escape and so-called victory the burial of
our own dead.   And he actually sneered at the
assumption that the King had been exposed to any
real danger in battle.   Nay, it is reported that in
his fury Pitt called Carteret "an execrable, a sole
minister, who had renounced the British nation, and
seemed to have drunk of the potion described in
poetic fictions which made men forget their country."

With all its exaggerations, Pitt's policy in the matter
was sound.   George II. and Carteret were indeed pursuing an aim which was not British, but Hanoverian.
Walpole himself might have made the speech with a
cooler judgment, more tolerance, and less violence.
But Pitt was here in substance the true English
statesman.

A few days later Pitt resumed his attack on the
whole Hanoverian policy.   His Majesty, he said, stood
on the brink of a precipice.   It was the duty of
Parliament to snatch him from that gulf where an
infamous minister had placed him.   The general of
the English army had not been consulted.   The great
person himself (the King) had been hemmed in by
German officers, and one English minister.   Every
symptom of some dreadful calamity attends the nation.

Again he said, "It would be happy for this country if the sober maxims and well-weighed councils of the Dutch government had an influence upon ours, which, he insinuated, were under the direction of a desperate and rodomontading minister." Mr. Gladstone never used such language of Mr. Disraeli in 1879, nor did Mr. Morley use such language of Lord Milner in 1899.

In January 1744 it was again proposed to vote £634,344 to send 21,000 men to Flanders to be employed in support of Maria Theresa. This Pitt opposed with his usual vehemence. He protested against continuing to assist the Queen of Hungary in a war with France, and especially against sending an army to Flanders. The scheme was so absurd that it must be a pretext to cover the maintenance of 16,000 Hanoverians and to add territory to the Electorate. *We should never assist our allies on the Continent with any great number of men—but only with our money and our ships.* We ought to have at home as few soldiers as possible. Soldiers are a danger to liberty.

How all this was to be reconciled with Pitt's invectives against Walpole, with his own acts as Prime Minister, and those of his son after him, is not self-evident. But whatever its inconsistency, Pitt's argument was the sound and patriotic policy. It was the policy of Walpole at his best. But now, strangely enough, the war policy of the King and Carteret was being assisted by the fallen minister in secret. Pitt was answered by Murray, the solicitor-general, but he held his ground with a high spirit, covering the Hanoverians with his sarcasms, and winding up with the truly Dantonesque trope that "the passing the question will be to erect a triumphal arch to Hanover over the military honour and independence of Great Britain."

It was of this famous duel between Pitt and the great Lord Mansfield (as Murray became) that James Oswald, Adam Smith's honest friend, wrote his well-known criticism. "The one spoke like a pleader, and could not divest himself of a certain appearance of having been employed by others. Pitt spoke like a gentleman, like a statesman, who felt what he said, and possessed the strongest desire of conveying that feeling to others, for their own interest, and that of their country. Murray *gains* your attention by the perspicuity of his arguments, and the elegance of his diction. Pitt *commands* your attention and respect by the nobleness, the greatness of his sentiments, the strength and energy of his expressions, and the certainty you are in of his always rising to a greater elevation both of thought and style. For this talent he possesses beyond any speaker I ever heard, of never falling from the beginning to the end of his speech, either in thought or expression. . . . I think him sincerely the most finished character I ever knew."

That Pitt was no factious place-hunter is sufficiently proved by his conduct at the great Jacobite raid. In February 1744 it was clear that England was threatened with a serious French invasion, in conjunction with a rising on behalf of the Stuart Pretender. Pelham moved an address to the King to raise such forces by sea and land as he might think necessary. Pitt supported this new military increase with all the passion that he had just poured on the expedition to Flanders.

He did not believe there was any real danger, but he heartily supported the minister in taking all needful precautions. In fact, a French force of 7000 actually sailed, but they were driven back by the weather at sea, and the Pretender had to adjourn his enterprise. In March, Louis XV. declared war in earnest. One hundred thousand men under Marshal Saxe carried all before them in Flanders, and the British and their allies were completely overpowered. Public indignation drove from office Lord Carteret, who had now become Lord Granville, but he still retained the confidence of the King.

The Pelhams were now masters of the situation, and proceeded to form a broad ministry so as to include the Patriots and the Cousinhood of the Temples. But all their efforts failed to shake the rooted antipathy of the King to Pitt, though he now detached himself from the Prince of Wales. He was left out in the cold, though Lyttelton and George Grenville were admitted. The hostility of the Court only added to Pitt's popularity with the public. Sarah, the old Duchess of Marlborough, by her will left him the sum of £10,000 "upon account of his merit, in the noble defence he has made for the support of the laws of England, and to prevent the ruin of his country." The money was sorely needed by the almost penniless patriot, and of course the wits attributed the change in his attitude to his accession of fortune. It did indeed require no little explanation to justify the change, when, in January 1745, Pitt supported the government in their demand for 28,000 men to be employed in Flanders.

He was ill with the gout; but, in flannels and on crutches, he came down to the House and opened a grandiloquent oration that, if this were to be the last day of his life, he would spend it in the House of Commons, for he thought the state of the country was even worse than that of his own health. As the House listened with patience to this tragic opening from a man of thirty-seven, he went on to say how greatly the whole situation had been changed by the retirement of Lord Carteret-Granville. He inveighed against "that fatal influence," multiplying war on war in romantic schemes of conquest to benefit Austria, but not Great Britain. He rehearsed all the misdeeds of Carteret, whom not ten men in all the nation would follow. But he had confidence in Mr. Pelham, his patriotism and his capacity, and believed him to be now pursuing moderate and healing measures. "He thought a dawn of salvation to this country had broken forth, and was determined to follow it as far as it would lead him. . . . Should he find himself deceived, nothing would be left but to act with an honest despair." All that needs to be said about this memorable conversion is, that Carteret-Granville, who knew more about the state of Europe than Pitt, or any other Englishman, was essentially reckless, visionary, and arrogant, whilst Henry Pelham was cautious, practical, and moderate. And the dangers to England, which were distant and unreal when George II. first began to meddle in the Austrian succession, had become very real and very close when France had prepared to invade us, when Charles Stuart was hovering over Scotland, and a Jacobite rising was imminent in England.

During the Scotch rebellion of 1745, which might
have been serious if the French had landed their force,
and if the Pretender had possessed real energy and
skill, Pitt stood firmly by the government, and showed
ardent loyalty to the Hanoverian dynasty. This
patriot, and favourite of the people, resisted a crude
proposal for parliamentary reform. "Is it now a
time," he said, "to sit contriving bills to guard our
liberties from corruption, when that very liberty,
when everything else dear to us, are in danger of
being wrested from us in arms? When thieves have
burst into the mansion, the fool only would plan out
methods to prevent the fraud of his servants." In
fact, Pitt had now definitely become a friend to the
ministry in which the two Pelhams were the predominant power. He paid compliments to Henry
Pelham, and profuse court to the Duke, his brother.

The Duke of Newcastle had irritated the King by
pressing on him the appointment of Pitt as secretary
of war, and George, who had never liked or trusted
his present ministers, tried a *coup de main* by recalling
Granville and Bath, *i.e.* Carteret and Pulteney. Their
forty-eight hours ministry vanished in air before the
country knew of its existence. The Pelhams returned
stronger than ever. This time, they insisted on having
Pitt as their colleague. Others who were his political
opponents joined in the same advice. Horace Walpole,
Lord Orford's younger brother, even drew up a memorial
to the King to show the importance of making Pitt
secretary of war. At last the King gave way. He
insisted that he would not have such a man about
his person. And Pitt, with unusual humility, pro-

tested that he did not seek to enter the royal closet. At last, it was the 22nd February 1745, Pitt was appointed Paymaster and Treasurer of War in Ireland. On the 6th of February following he was appointed Paymaster in England. He was now thirty-eight, and had been eleven years in the House of Commons. Horace Walpole wrote that he had taken the place "by storm."

This subordinate office is remarkable chiefly for the public proof it gave of Pitt's integrity. The age, it has been said, was one in which anything short of actual embezzlement of public money was regarded as fair in the game of party preferment. No one has ever shown whence Walpole derived the enormous sums he spent on Houghton. Henry Fox, Pitt's contemporary and rival, notoriously amassed a large fortune from office. The practice in the Paymaster's Office had long been to retain £100,000 in advance, which brought an annual return of several thousand pounds to the private purse of the fortunate holder. It was considered that so lucrative an appointment would console Pitt for his exclusion from the Cabinet. He was a poor man, who long lived on the bounty of others; at the same time he was extravagant and ostentatious to the point of ridicule. But he utterly refused to touch a penny of the interest on this £100,000, or anything beyond his legal salary.

Again, it was usual, when Parliament granted subsidies to a foreign power, for the Paymaster to receive a *douceur* of one-half per cent. as his perquisite. This degrading practice, sanctioned by the most respectable of his predecessors, revolted the spirit of Pitt. To

have yielded to it would soon have placed him in
great wealth. He rigidly refused to avail himself
of the rule. When a subsidy was voted to the King
of Sardinia, Pitt declined to retain the usual commission. The foreign king, with many expressions of
admiration, begged to be allowed to offer him the
amount as a royal present from himself. This Pitt
firmly and respectfully declined. On no occasion was
he even suspected of the slightest attempt to benefit
by his official trust. And his absolute integrity
throughout his public career is vouched for by his
enemies and his satirists. Pitt was not the man to
let his burning zeal for public duty remain under
a bushel. It greatly enhanced his reputation in the
nation. But it stands recorded that Chatham was
the first great statesman to extinguish that curse of
corruption which had afflicted English politics since
the Restoration, as William Pitt, the son, was the
statesman who finally established strict honour in the
public service.

CHAPTER V

IN SUBORDINATE OFFICE

THE ten years that passed from Pitt's attaining to subordinate office until he was at last admitted to the Cabinet, formed a time of petty intrigues at home, European complications abroad, inglorious war, and public discontent. It is the period of Pitt's career which is marked by his most glaring inconsistencies, wherein it is least possible to acquit him of factious manœuvres and a purely self-interested ambition. He thirsted for power, not for money nor for influence, but with a gnawing passion to be able to carry out his great designs, and to put an end to the sordid bungling of his official chiefs. He found the way barred to him by the personal antipathy of the King and the jealous rivalry of the oligarchic clans. He would yield neither to the Court nor to the magnates; he would hold firm to the nation, not to its sovereign; he would stand by his own independence, and never sink to be a docile placeman. In this dilemma, he struck out right and left at the Ministry he now served, or at the Opposition he had now quitted, as for the time it seemed to offer a chance for his forcing his way to power, for his making the official parties fear his attacks, or for convincing the King at last that he was indispensable. If his conduct was dishonourable, it was the kind of dishonour with which all English politicians have been charged, and of which few have been entirely guiltless. I shall not attempt the task of defending all these manœuvres. I shall state them fairly, not seeking to palliate them, nor pretending to judge them from a true standard of honour and patriotism.

It can hardly be gainsaid that Pitt was now resolved to throw himself heartily into the party of the Pelhams. Henry Pelham was a man of sense and character, a mild edition of Walpole, with a timid wish to carry on much the same policy. His brother, the Duke, was an arch time-server, whose secret purpose was to gain the favour of the King In the result King George managed to continue the Hanoverian policy of subsidies, wars, and European imbroglios. And in effect Pitt, who held a minor office without any control of general policy, is found to be passionately advocating what was practically the very system he had so long denounced. His eulogist tries to show that, feeling himself powerless to resist, Pitt consented to remain silent. But he did not at all remain silent or obscure. His eloquence, he being the tool of Newcastle, who was the tool of the King, carried through Parliament the very measures he used to assail. There are some excuses for this desertion of all the principles on which his great reputation had been based. The Jacobite rising, a French war and prospect of invasion, had thoroughly roused him to the need of supporting the old Whig connection. He had become a warm friend to the Hanoverian dynasty, had parted with a

factious Prince of Wales, and had attached himself to
the fighting Duke of Cumberland. The foreign policy
of Pelham, in spite of all its subsidies and treaties, was
a totally different thing from that of Carteret. It was
much less wanton, and had more purpose and excuse.
These things may have enabled Pitt to persuade himself that he was acting in good conscience. They are
not enough to acquit him at the bar of history of time-
serving and insincerity.

However subordinate and detached was the office he
held, he was the greatest living force in debate, and
the ministry relied on his support. Pelham told his
brother, the Duke, that Pitt had the dignity of Wyndham, the wit of Pulteney, the knowledge and judgment of Walpole. It needed, indeed, a preposterous
compliment to explain away Pitt's supporting the payment of 18,000 Hanoverians in Flanders; his defending the treaties with Spain and Bavaria; his recanting
his resistance to the Spanish "right of search." All
that can be said of this is, that he loudly asserted now
that he had been entirely wrong. The one thing he
would not surrender was his resistance to any reduction of the fleet. He opposed the government on this
point, as he constantly did, but he did so with profuse
protestations of his devotion to the great party to
which he said he would hold on through life. Here
again is a mark that all Pitt's inmost hopes and ideals
lay beyond the narrow seas. He could play fast and
loose with European politics. He was ever true to his
pursuit of Sea Power. "The sea is our natural
element," he had said in his great speech of 1744
against the expedition to Flanders.

From this time begins the long rivalry between Pitt
and Henry Fox, such as was renewed between their
sons half a century later.   Both Pitt and Fox were
straining every nerve to gain power—Fox all wit,
adroitness, cynicism, and greed; Pitt all passion,
patriotism, arrogance, and indiscretion.   For the
moment both found it their interest to rally round the
Pelhams and support the cause of the King.   Pitt was
now an ardent ministerialist—be the measures under
debate large or small, old or new, liberal or tory.   The
acute and cool Pelham wrote again to Newcastle, "I
think him (Pitt) the most able and useful man we
have amongst us; truly honourable and strictly
honest."   Was it a bill to subject half-pay navy
officers to martial law ?—Pitt supported it !   The "New
Mutiny Bill" subjected half-pay soldiers to martial
law.   Pitt supported the clause with his usual fury.
"We must trust to the virtue of the army : without
this virtue, even should the Lords, the Commons, and
the people of England entrench themselves behind
parchment up to the teeth, the sword will find a
passage to the vitals of the Constitution."   It is not
easy to see where the vitals of the Constitution come
in.   But in the heroic, or what Horace Walpole called
the Pittic, style, the Bill seemed big with military
despotism.   Pitt was willing to risk this in reliance on
"the virtue" of our army.   He did not remember that
but a year or two before he had thundered out that
"the man who solely depends upon arms for bread,
can never be a good subject, especially in a free
country."

Did the ministers propose a grant of £10,000 to the

City of Glasgow to indemnify it from the exactions
made by the Pretender in 1745, whilst they left
Carlisle and Derby without compensation?   The
thunder of Pitt again resounded through the House
in support of the grant.   "I am shocked, Sir, that
such a question should stand a debate in a British
House of Commons.   Had the rebels succeeded in
their flagitious attempt, and called a slavish Parliament, I should not have wondered to see such a question opposed in a House of Commons assembled by
their authority."   And so forth in a long and passionate speech, calling all who opposed him Jacobites,
ending with, "Their ruin must be inevitable, or the
relief must be granted!"   All this about a grant of
£10,000 to the corporation of a city, the valuation of
which is now some five millions sterling.   The "march
to Derby" and the French invasion made a real
revolution in British politics; but one of its incidental
effects was to make Pitt the first lieutenant of the
Pelhams, and for the time even "a King's man."

When it was moved that no soldier should be
punished unless by court-martial, Pitt, even in this
"free country," would not hear of the conduct of the
army or soldiers' complaints being mentioned in Parliament.   "We have no business with such matters;
those are subjects which belong to the King."   Did
Lord Egmont, now "the Prince's man," move for
papers relating to the demolition of Dunkirk, Pitt
defended the ministry for refusing them.   "It was not
only impolitic, but dangerous, tending to involve the
nation in another war with France."   The fire-eating
and terrible cornet of horse now had a conscientious

horror of war such as Walpole might have envied.
The Peace of Aix-la-Chapelle was "absolutely necessary for our very being."

In January 1751 Pitt made a speech in favour of the
annual subsidy of £40,000 to the Elector of Bavaria.
"The treaty with Bavaria was founded in the best
political wisdom; it was a wise measure, tending most
effectually to preserve the balance of power in
Germany, and of course the tranquillity of Europe."
"The treaty with Spain was a wise and advantageous
measure." Lord Egmont, an opposition leader, reminded him that this wise treaty made no mention of
the British resistance to the right of search. Yes!
said Pitt, he had once been for *No Search*—"but he
was a young man then; he was now ten years older,
and considered public affairs more coolly"; and now
he saw that the claim for *No Search* could not be
maintained against Spain. Pitt never, at any time of
his life, considered things *coolly*, unless this astounding
avowal may be considered "cool." *Tempora mutantur*
(*i.e.* administrations) *nos et mutamur in illis.* In one
thing only did Pitt not change his coat to please a
minister. The government asked for 8000 seamen for
the year. Motion made for a vote of 10,000. Pitt
supported the amendment, minister as he was himself,
and Paymaster. "The fleet," said he in his grandiose
way, "the fleet is our standing army." Pitt was the
Captain Mahan of his own age.

The petty struggle went on now with three principal factions—first, the Pelhams together with Pitt;
then, the Duke of Bedford's party, with the Duke of
Cumberland and Fox; thirdly, the Prince of Wales's

set, with Lord Bute, Lord Egmont, and the wrecked genius of Lord Bolingbroke—him whom Pitt once spoke of as "the late Bolingbroke of impious memory." The sudden death of the Prince in March 1751 caused a new shuffling of the cards. As the young George was but twelve, a Regency Bill became urgent. The struggle took place between the partisans of the Princess Mother and those of the Duke of Cumberland. Pitt stood by the Princess, Fox stood by the Duke; and a lively oratorical duel resulted, in which it would seem that Pitt had the best of it both in temper and in eloquence.

The Prince's death and the Regency Act so completely shattered the opposition that the Pelhams contrived to get rid of the Duke of Bedford and his followers, and actually made the once fiery and brilliant Carteret-Granville President of the Council. Pitt's "execrable minister" was now an extinct volcano and a drunkard; and Pitt and he had no difficulty in remaining peaceful colleagues. For some time the Pelham administration led the most tranquil existence ever known to Parliament—Henry Pelham, timid, moderate, wise; the Duke, his brother, restless in petty manœuvres; Pitt, Fox, Murray, all supporting the government for the hour, while each aspired to succeed it. In the midst of the calm, Henry Pelham, a strong man of sixty, was carried off by a sudden attack.

The wild struggles for place which thereupon ensued fill many a lively page in the memoirs and correspondence of the time. Pitt was at Bath very ill of the gout; but he wrote to his friend Lyttelton, urging him to push his claims to Hardwicke, the Chancellor, "whose wisdom, firmness, and authority" he extols. He wrote imploringly to Newcastle as the "unalterable humble servant to your Grace." The overbearing Pitt indeed now prostrated himself before all who held the keys to the Cabinet. It was in vain. The King was inexorable. All Pitt's passionate advocacy of the subsidies, all his defence of the Hanoverian dynasty, could not wash out the old affronts. Pitt might overawe the House of Commons, but he had neither party nor clan at his back. Newcastle wanted him as a colleague, but he feared him as a rival ; Lyttelton, from misunderstanding or jealousy, served Pitt but ill, and they became bitterly estranged when Lyttelton and Grenville were taken and Pitt was left outside the Council.

Pitt was deeply mortified. He wrote to Newcastle a letter full of pride and despair. He was manifestly excluded from office, he said, by a personal veto. He had no wish but to retreat—"Not a retreat of resentment, but of respect, and of despair of being ever accepted to equal terms with others, be his poor endeavours what they may." Very few had been the honours and advantages of his life. He hopes that some. retreat neither dishonourable nor disagreeable may be opened to him. To Lord Hardwicke he wrote : "My Lord, after having set out under suggestions of this general hope ten years ago and bearing long a load of obloquy for supporting the King's measures, and never obtaining in recompense the smallest remission of that displeasure I vainly laboured to soften, all ardour for public business is really extinguished in my mind, and I am totally deprived of all consideration by which alone I could have been of any use. The weight of irremovable royal displeasure is a load too great to move under: it must crush any man; it has sunk and broke me." Let those who are ready to sneer at Pitt's humiliation and to moralise over his ambition, think of "whatever records may leap to light," when the private letters of the politicians of our own age will ultimately be given to the world.

'Tis pitiful reading these letters of Pitt to his friends and the ministers all through these months of March, April, and May. He was detained at Bath, racked with pain, hardly able to stand, to write, or be carried about. He was bursting with desire to be Secretary of State and to lead the House of Commons, to which he justly thought himself entitled. He could not move from his invalid chair, and he wrote with his lame hand illegible scrawls to George Grenville, to Lyttelton, to Lord Temple, urging tactics, a plan to force their claims on the Court, on the Chancellor, and on the Duke, "to talk modestly, to fish in the troubled waters, to act like public men in a dangerous conjuncture for our country." In the meantime Lord Temple was to rally the Cousinhood, muster their friends in Parliament, and make the magnates understand that they must satisfy their claims or prepare for their hostility. It is not very lofty, nor quite in the vein of Aristides and Cato. But it is what is often done (they say) even to-day, in a ministerial crisis.

The shifty Duke of Newcastle contrived to be

E

Prime Minister himself, and put in his creature, a dull respectability, Sir T. Robinson, to lead the House. " He might as well send us his jackboot to lead us," said Pitt. But this manœuvre cost him the angry opposition of Pitt and of Fox, as soon as a new Parliament was elected, and even for a time, a sort of coalition of Pitt with Fox, in combined opposition. Pitt retained his office, as Fox did his ; but neither of them thought this any reason for abstaining to attack Sir Thomas, as often as they chose. A more useful public service was the new Chelsea Pensioners Relief Act, which Pitt devised and carried, to protect the poor old soldiers from the scandalous extortions to which they were exposed.

Pitt was not long in formally attacking the Duke himself. It was one of his most famous outbursts ; and, by good fortune, we have accounts of it from two most competent, though both unfriendly, sources—no less than Fox himself and Horace Walpole. In a letter to Lord Hartington, Fox says : "It was the finest speech that ever Pitt spoke, and, perhaps, the most remarkable." A young member, whose seat was attacked for bribery, treated the accusation with "buffoonery, which kept the House in a continual roar of laughter. Mr. Pitt came down from the gallery, and took it up in his highest tone of dignity. He was astonished when he heard what had been the occasion of their mirth. Was the dignity of the House of Commons on so sure foundation, that they might venture themselves to shake it ? Had it not been diminishing for years, till now we were brought to the very brink of the precipice where, if ever, a stand must be made? High compliments to the Speaker, eloquent exhortation to Whigs of all conditions, to defend their attacked and expiring liberty, etc. Unless you will degenerate into a little assembly, serving no other purpose than to register the arbitrary decrees of one too powerful subject (laying on the words *one* and *subject* the most remarkable emphasis)." So writes Fox. Horace Walpole tells it in almost the same words, and adds: "This thunderbolt, thrown in a sky so long serene, confounded the audience. Murray crouched, silent and terrified," etc. etc. "It was observed," wrote Fox, "that by his first two periods, he brought the House to a silence and attention, that you might have heard a pin drop." And Fox adds that the Duke of Newcastle was in the utmost fidget, and that "it spoiled his stomach." But the craven minister, thus flouted by his subordinate, dared not call for his dismissal.

Pitt and Fox both continued to pour heavy shot into the Duke and his Chancellor of the Exchequer. Then Pitt turned on Murray (the future Lord Mansfield, and a great Judge). Fox wrote: "I sate next Murray; *who suffered for an hour.*" Though the Duke dared not dismiss Pitt, he saw that he must detach him from Fox. Thereupon a mysterious three-cornered game of *finesse* took place between Newcastle with Hardwicke, Fox and the Duke of Cumberland, and Pitt by himself. In the end, Newcastle induced Fox to leave Pitt, and enter the Cabinet. Pitt's friends and eulogists praise his dignity and self-command. Fox's friends say the same of him, with cross-accusations of the other side. Whatever may be the whole truth, Pitt considered that he had been left in the lurch, and he never forgave Fox, though it is far from clear that Fox had played him false, or had ever pledged himself to be his friend. Pitt said he would not serve *under* Fox; but added, they would not quarrel.

Newcastle still tried to pacify Pitt without admitting him to the Council. He sent the elder Horace Walpole to him: on which Pitt told the Duke flatly that he expected cabinet office at the first vacancy. When Lord Hardwicke's son, Charles Yorke, went to Pitt with protestations from the Duke of friendship and confidence, Pitt cut him short, and said friendship and confidence there was none between them; if there ever had been, it was at an end. He would take nothing as a favour from his Grace. The Duke tried a third envoy, the illustrious Chancellor in person. Pitt was obdurate. He would have no subsidies, nor give any foreign power aid, unless Hanover was attacked owing to its sovereign being England's King. One subsidy he might consent to support: two would be as bad as twenty. He would not accept "a system" of subsidies. Pitt was still fiercely defying the King and the government. He was still Paymaster of the Forces; and the Prime Minister did not have the courage to call for his resignation. Ministerial joint responsibility is said to be lax to-day. It evidently had not begun to exist in those times.

But at last, in November 1755, the cup was full. On the address Pitt rose after uninteresting discourses, Horace Walpole tells us: "his eloquence, like a torrent long obstructed, burst forth with more commanding impetuosity—haughty, defiant, conscious of injury, and of supreme abilities." He inveighed against the use of the King's sacred name in Parliament. He had long seen the dignity of the House dwindling, sinking. He asked, must we drain our last vital drop and send it to the North Pole ? (A squadron was going to the Baltic.) He protested again and again against burdening England with the interests of Hanover. They talk of the law of nations, but Nature is the best writer—she will teach us to be men, and not truckle to power. "I, who travel through a desert, and am overwhelmed with mountains of obscurity, cannot catch a gleam to direct me to the beauties of these negotiations." And then he burst into the famous simile of the Rhone and the Saône (which seems to us to-day merely a bit of rhetoric, and not at all the true fire of the real Pitt).[1]

He continued that "these incoherent, un-British measures were adopted in place of our proper force— our navy. Were these treaties English measures ? were they preventive measures ? were they not measures of aggression ? Would they not provoke Prussia, and light up a general war ? All our misfortunes were owing to those daring, wicked councils. He could imagine the King abroad surrounded by affrighted Hanoverians, with no advocate for England near him. Within two years his Majesty would not

---

[1] "I remember that at Lyons I was taken to see the conflux of the Rhone and the Saône—the one a gentle, feeble, languid stream, and though languid, of no great depth ; the other a boisterous and impetuous torrent ; but different as they are they meet at last—and long may they continue united, to the comfort of each other, and to the glory, honour, and security of their nation."

be able to sleep in St. James's for the cries of a bankrupt people." This was too much even for Newcastle.
Pitt was dismissed from his place. With him too
went his allies, Legge and George Grenville.

To some it seemed that Pitt, now a man long past
middle life, now a third time debarred from power, in
a hopeless minority, almost friendless, penniless, a confirmed invalid, tortured with gout, and forced to resort
to long spells of retirement, was finally to be reckoned
a political ruin. It was not so. Within twelve months
he was First Minister of King George, and the head
of the most powerful government of the eighteenth
century.

It was in the midst of these public cares that there
came to Pitt almost the one perfectly unclouded happiness of his stormy life—his marriage to Lady Hester
Grenville, the only sister of his friend, Earl Temple.
It seems to have been a rather sudden engagement,
followed immediately by marriage, which took place
on 15th November 1754, a few months after his terrible
illness at Bath. The only sister of his intimate friends,
the Grenvilles, the cousin of George Lyttelton and of
Thomas Pitt's wife, had of course been known to Pitt
from her childhood. He was himself a bachelor of
mature age, and he was married on his own forty-sixth
birthday. Lady Hester lived into the nineteenth
century, until nearly half a century after this date,
and she was a young woman at marriage. She seems
to have possessed grace, virtue, and good sense in
abundance. Assuredly the marriage proved to be one
of unalloyed happiness and mutual affection. Nothing
in Pitt's whole life was a more perfect success.

By the fresh alliance with the wealthy and powerful
family seated at Stowe, Pitt greatly strengthened his
political position. His wife brought him every happiness that a good and able woman could bring to the
husband she adored. They had two daughters, beside
three sons, of whom the second was William, the illustrious Prime Minister of George III. There is not a
cloud or a defect in any aspect of Pitt's private life.
He was abstemious, affectionate, thoughtful, and generous. As Lord Brougham wrote—"To all his family
he was simple, kindly, and gentle." The archives
of Stowe have preserved for us the letters which
Earl Temple received from his sister and her future
husband. They are couched in the solemn (and to us
the stilted) style of that age. Lady Hester writes to
"her dearest brother," with "millions of thanks for
your love to him, to me." She feels "that pride and
pleasure in his partiality for me which his infinite
worth not only justifies, but renders right." Pitt on
his side tells Lord Temple, " You sent me from Stowe
the most blessed of men." He tells George Grenville,
the other brother, that he must "count every moment
till the world sees me the most honoured and blessed
of men!" Yes! they are what we now regard as
artificial and cumbrous for love-letters. But their
meaning is sound, warm, and true in feeling. The
form was that of the "polite-letter," it is true; but the
substance was sincerity, honour, and love.

The letters of Pitt have always been regarded as
stiff and awkward. The King said Pitt's letters were
affected, formal, and pedantic. He was not an adroit
penman ; and too much has been made of the anecdote

that he asked a young lawyer to correct his mistakes. Pitt was not a Horace Walpole, just as Horace Walpole was not a Pitt. The genius of the one lay in his pen, that of the other in his voice. But in substance the letters of Pitt are manly, dignified, wise, and wholesome. If one would know what Pitt was as a man, one should turn to his familiar letters to his nephew, the son of Thomas Pitt, and afterwards the first Lord Camelford. They were published exactly one hundred years ago in a dainty volume by Lord Grenville, George's son, who dedicated the collection to William Pitt, then Prime Minister, in 1804. The letters begin to "My dear Child" at Cambridge in 1751, when Pitt was struggling for office, and are continued until 1757, when he was first minister and the greatest personage in Europe.

We should call such letters to-day solemn common-place, affected erudition; but I confess to a real enjoyment in their affectionate interest in a promising lad, and in their keen zest for the old classical tags. This mature bachelor, the terrible gladiator of Parliament, writes long disquisitions on study to his brother's clever boy. He corrects his verse translation of the *Eclogues*. He insists on his going through the *Aeneid* from beginning to end. "God bless you, my dear child, your most affectionate uncle"—before whom, he might have added, Fox and Murray cower. "Love the *Iliad*, and Virgil particularly." "Drink as deep as you can of these divine springs—*ille impiger hausit spumantem pateram*," etc. etc. "He should fix on the curtains of his bed, and on the walls of his chamber, the maxim — *Vitanda est improba Siren,*

Desidia." Rise early, keep regular hours for study.
Your books should be Euclid, Logic, Experimental
Philosophy, Locke, Horace, Virgil, Tully, the history
of England, Burnet, Molière, Addison—there is nothing about Brunck or Schützius, or German erudition.
"If you are not right towards God, you can never be
so towards man—*ingratum qui dixerit, omnia dixit."*
"Remember the essence of religion is, a heart void of
offence towards God and man; not subtle speculative
opinions, but an active vital principle of faith."

Then follow precepts as to Behaviour—quite as
sound and less superficial than those addressed by
Lord Chesterfield to his son. Do not be above such
trifles as taking manly exercises with grace and
vigour. Do not give way to idle laughter, *risu inepto
res ineptior nulla est.* Politeness is "benevolence in
trifles." "I cannot tell you better how truly and
tenderly I love you, than by telling you I am most
solicitously bent on your doing everything that is
right," etc. etc. Stale truisms enough, in the style of
Thackeray's Colonel Newcome, but written by a man
racked with gout and hardly able to hold a pen, in the
midst of his great struggle with the Duke. In May
1754, after his bitter disappointment, he writes from
Bath with his lame hand as to a general course of
English History—Burnet, Bolingbroke, Bacon, Lord
Clarendon, May, and so forth—all sadly antiquated,
and not a word about original research in the Record
Office or the British Museum—but merely such
meagre compendiums as nourished the great genius
who made so much of English history.

In 1755 he writes from the Pay Office, praising his

nephew's remarks, "natural, manly, and sensible," on
some West Saxons, and on his declamation on the
thesis *Omne solum forti Patria est*—" a maxim that may
have supported some great and good men in exile,
Algernon Sidney, Ludlow—but what fatal casuistry
may lie therein, to such a villain as Bolingbroke." So
moralises the mature "Boy Patriot," who lived to be
the Veteran Patriot of the American War, he who has
ever on his lips the maxim—*ingenti patriae perculsus
amore*.

He continues his affectionate letters, and his scheme
of reading, after his own marriage and when his
nephew's academic career was closed. "I ever intend
learning as the weapon and instrument only of manly,
honourable, and virtuous action upon the stage of the
world." Again he writes as to history, mentioning
Lady Hester and her child, or again, he mentions in a
characteristic sentence— "*Finitimus Oratori Poeta.*"
"Substitute Tully and Demosthenes in the place of
Homer and Virgil; and arm yourself with all the
variety of manner, copiousness and beauty of diction,
nobleness and magnificence of ideas of the Roman
consul, and the close and forcible reasoning, the depth
and fortitude of mind of the Grecian statesman."
Even in the intimacy of family life, Pitt's mind ever
turned to the memory of Demosthenes. These familiar
letters have not the sparkling wit of Horace Walpole,
nor the pellucid incisiveness of Chesterfield. They
are ponderous in form and trite in expression; but
they come from a greater nature, and picture to us a
loftier ideal.

CHAPTER VI

FIRST MINISTRY

THE month of November 1755 found Henry Fox the Leader in the House of Commons; Newcastle, still the head of a discredited government in a national crisis, full of disasters at sea and on land; and Pitt, Legge, and George Grenville dismissed from their offices, having long been in opposition to a chaotic administration. Pitt was now resolved, not simply to be admitted to the ministry, but to supersede it. And he took care to explain to the nation and to public men the policy which he intended to enforce. His pecuniary condition was gloomy. Deprived of his salary, without hereditary fortune (and he had strictly resisted the temptation to make any profit out of his official opportunities), married to a lady of title but not of wealth, Pitt was unable to maintain a suitable position.

In this emergency, Lord Temple came to the rescue with great generosity; and the correspondence between him, his sister, and his brother-in-law is so characteristic of the persons concerned and of the Grandisonian style of the age, that we may give it in their own words. On the very day of Pitt's dismissal

(20th November), Earl Temple writes to Lady Hester Pitt :—

"MY DEAR LADY HESTER,—I cannot defer till to-morrow morning making a request to you upon the success of which I have so entirely set my heart, that I flatter myself you will not refuse it me. I must entreat you to make use of all your interest with Mr. Pitt to give his brother Temple leave to become his debtor for a thousand pounds a year till better times. Mr. P. will never have it in his power to confer so great an obligation upon, dear Lady Hester, your most truly affectionate brother, TEMPLE."

Lady Hester writes from her bed (her first child, the future Lady Stanhope, was hardly a month old) in the vein of the "accomplished Miss Byron," to assure her dear brother how highly she is his obliged and most affectionate sister. Pitt to his credit frankly accepted the generous offer. Lord Temple writes to his sister that he is infinitely happy: "This proof of his kindness and friendship to me is the only remaining one that he could give me." "How decline, or how receive so great a generosity so amiably offered," writes Pitt, "to the best and noblest of brothers?" A correspondence which, in spite of formalities and compliments, does honour to all three.

Though now in fierce opposition to his late colleagues, there was nothing really factious in Pitt's attitude. He held the situation of the country to be desperately bad, the ministers to be incapable, himself to be at once inevitable and indispensable; but he was willing to support any measures that were needed by the country, until he should be called to power. Though he still sat in Parliament for what was called one of Newcastle's boroughs, he did not consider that

any reason for holding his peace. It is indeed to his
honour that he declined to recognise any allegiance to
the Duke, who had so long made use of his services
whilst excluding him from office.

Accordingly, Pitt supported an amendment to raise
the seamen for the ensuing year to 50,000. He
shuddered that our resources for the sea service were
so narrow. He recalled the fatal reduction of 1751
to 8000. He would pursue the authors of such
measures as make the King's Crown totter on his
head. Never was a noble country so perniciously
neglected, so undone by the silly pride of one man,
or the timidity of his colleagues. Broad shame stared
them in the face. Shame and danger had come together. He concluded with a prayer for the King,
for his posterity, for this poor, forlorn, distressed
country.

When the secretary at war moved to add 15,000
men to the army, Pitt seconded the motion with
ardour. Our whole force was necessary. It was not
enough to send two miserable battalions as victims to
America. He wished to alarm the nation, to make the
danger reach the ears of his Majesty. He turned from
the venerable age of the King to his grandson *born an
Englishman*. He drew a picture of a French invasion
of London and the horrors ensuing. How could men
so guilty face their countrymen ? The decay of the
country was caused by the little spirit of domination,
the ambition of being the only figure amongst cyphers
—[Newcastle (1), Fox (0), Lyttelton (0), etc., etc.,
etc. (0).] He wanted to call the country out of that
nerveless state, that 20,000 men from France could

shake it. He wished to see that breed revived which had carried our glory so high. It needed no Burleigh, no Richelieu to have foreseen all that had happened. He did not ask for the punishment of ministers. Our calamities no doubt were owing to the weakness of their heads, not to their evil intent.

Before the year (1755) had ended, Pitt moved his famous scheme for a militia:—a half-trained territorial army of 60,000—with a standing army never less than 18,000. They would be exercised on Sundays and one other day in the week for 110 days, at 6d. per day—with no deductions. The officers to have no pay, but to be drawn from the landed gentry —four sergeants (from the regular army) to each eighty men—the total cost under £300,000. Really a clear, practicable, well-thought scheme which Pitt ultimately carried out when in power. All through the session Pitt constantly attacked Fox and poured out scorn on Newcastle, even professing his honour for Sir Robert Walpole, whom he respected—after his fall —what! do any laugh?—was it not more honourable to respect a man after his fall, than when he was all-powerful? "Sir Robert," said Pitt, "thought well of me, died in peace with me." "He was a truly English Minister, he withstood Hanover, and kept a strict hand on the closet."

When treaties with Russia and Hesse and Prussia were submitted to Parliament, Pitt opposed. He opposed the grant for the Hanoverian troops. This was not an administration, he said. "They shift and shuffle the charge from one to another. Says one, I am not general. The treasury says, I am not

admiral.   The admiralty says, I am not minister.
From such an unaccording assemblage of separate
and distinct powers with no system, a nullity results.
One, two, three, four, five lords meet—if they cannot
agree:—Oh! we will meet again on Saturday.   Oh!
but, says one of them, I am to go out of town."   Such
was a cabinet council in 1756.   We trust nothing like
it ever did or could occur in 1904.

When the country was seething with panic about
a French invasion and the expected loss of Minorca,
Pitt thundered again at the feeble and distracted
ministry.   We had provoked before we were able to
defend, and had neglected defence after the provoca-
tion.   He would not have signed the treaty with
Prussia for the five great places held by those who
signed it.   If he saw a child (the Duke of Newcastle) driving a go-cart on a precipice, with that
precious freight of an old king and his family, surely
he was bound to take the reins from his hands.   He
prayed to God that his Majesty might not have
Minorca, like Calais, written on his heart!

Minorca, as we know, was lost.   The unlucky Byng
made a poor fight with the French and sailed away in
the night, though he had more ships than the enemy.
Calcutta was stormed by the Nawab of Bengal, and
the British prisoners were stifled in the Black Hole.
The French in Canada captured Oswego on Lake
Ontario, with 1200 prisoners, 130 cannon, stores,
ammunition, two sloops, and 200 barges.   The country
was in a tempest of indignation, and in fact these
disasters were all primarily due to ministerial blundering and inaction.   The child driving the go-cart now

saw the precipice, which at any rate confronted himself.
He saw that his time was come. Fox deserted him,
and offered a coalition with Pitt, which was the desire
of the King. "You mean you will not act with me
as minister?" asked Fox. "I do," said Pitt. The
agitation was intense. The King was in alarm, talked
about Pitt sending him to the Tower. The Duke of
Devonshire, an honest neutral, was summoned to form
a ministry, as Dukes of Devonshire both then and now
usually are summoned in a crisis. Pitt "behaved with
haughty warmth"; stated his own terms; Newcastle
must be entirely out of it; Fox also; he must name
the places for his own friends; but, says Walpole, he
wanted friends for places more than places for friends.
Pitt found it difficult to place his demands before the
King, who would not see him. So, for the first time
in his life, he went to Lady Yarmouth, the King's
German mistress, with whom Newcastle, Fox, Hardwicke, and the rest were in regular communication.
The visit was noted as singular, only in that he had
never been to her before. Popular addresses for a
new ministry continued to pour in. The City of
London demanded to have supplies stopped. A wild
scramble ensued, delightfully and maliciously told by
Horace Walpole, who quotes Addison's remark on
Virgil that "*Pitt tossed about his dirt with an air of
majesty.*"

At last, after infinite manœuvring by Fox, Newcastle,
and minor men, a ministry was formed, nominally
under the Duke of Devonshire, with Pitt "First
Minister," as Walpole says; Lord Temple, at the
Admiralty; Mr. Legge, Chancellor of the Exchequer;

and George Grenville, Treasurer of the Navy. What
with Pitt's haughtiness, and his indifference to anything but foreign affairs, says Walpole, the Duke
retained the patronage whilst Pitt had the power.
But he remained prostrated with gout all the winter.
He had no accession of new friends but from the
Tories who hated Fox. And an inveterate paper
war was opened with unlimited abuse directed at his
gout and his supposed new friends. In truth, he
had not now, and never had, any political friend but
himself.

Pitt was now in high office, but hardly yet in power.
His difficulties were extreme, his hold precarious, and
his enemies unbroken. He had, says Carlyle, all
England at his back; but he had the King, the Duke
of Cumberland, the great magnates against him; Fox,
the Duke of Newcastle, and the bulk of the Parliament
Whigs plotting to ruin him. The old gang, who with
Newcastle and Fox had formed what Horace Walpole
called the worst administration in his memory, still
retained their offices and embarrassed their chief.

The condition of the country was as bad. After
half a century of possession, Minorca had been lost
to the French; a British army had capitulated; and
a British fleet had been disgraced. The Seven Years'
War had begun. France, Austria, Russia, with Saxony
and Sweden, were at last united to crush Prussia—
ninety millions against five. They threatened Hanover,
the King's German dominion; for George was now at
last the ally of Frederick. England was at war with
France, which threatened to become paramount in the
whole North American continent. The treaty of Aix-

la-Chapelle, which had restored the island of Cape
Breton to France, had omitted to define the boundaries
that separated the peninsula of Nova Scotia from
Canada proper. For years a bitter and irregular
struggle had been carried on between the French and
the British settlers in North America. The British
colonists were said to number 1,200,000; the French
about 52,000. But the British were unorganised in
separate colonies, with distinct governments, and had
very slight help from the mother country; the French
had a single rule, competent soldiers from France, and
a chain of well-placed forts.

France now boldly asserted her claim to the whole
valley of the St. Lawrence and its tributaries, and to
the whole valley of the Mississippi and its tributaries.
She insisted on hemming in the British to the Atlantic
seaboard, east of the Alleghany Mountains. That is
to say, that except Newfoundland, Nova Scotia, and
what are now the Eastern States, the whole North
American continent was to be French; and this,
though the colonists numbered but one in twenty-
four of the British. The French had secured the
support of the principal Indian tribes. The defeat
and death of Braddock, the capture of British stockades
and settlements, and the small results of the fleet
sent out to intercept the reinforcements from France,
seemed to portend that the British colonies were to
be hemmed in along the coast. France now blocked
their extension to the north, to the west, and to the
south. Had this ambitious vision of French statesmen ultimately succeeded, the English language would
not be spoken to-day throughout the vast American

continent on any more territory than the strip between the sea and the Blue Mountains, little more than three hundred miles broad. The issue—one of the most momentous in modern history—was determined otherwise by the energy and genius of one man.

It has been well said that for some years the biography of Pitt is to be read in the history of the world. His influence was felt in Europe, in India, in Africa, in America : from the Baltic to the St. Lawrence, from the Mediterranean to Bengal—for a time even more potent than that of Frederick himself—inasmuch as Pitt controlled the greatest sea-power in the world, and thoroughly understood its ubiquitous force. If Frederick had been crushed in the Seven Years' War, Central Europe would have become the prey of Russia, Austria, and France. And Frederick well knew what he owed to Pitt. As the King of Prussia wrote—"C'était la meilleure tête de l'Angleterre." Had Dupleix been able to extend and consolidate the empire he was so near founding in Madras, France, and not England, might have become the suzerain of Hindustan. If Montcalm had succeeded in establishing the French control of the St. Lawrence, the Lakes, and the Mississippi valley, France, not Britain, would have been the mother country of America. How different would the aspect of the world be to-day! In 1755, all these three possible results were far from improbable. In 1761, they had become utterly impossible.

The biography of Pitt in these years has to be read in the history of the world, a history which it is obvious cannot be even sketched in outline in these pages. All that can be done here is to note the occasions wherein is visible the master-hand of the British statesman. During the year 1757, Pitt was hardly master of his own government. The ejected ministers still retained a dominant influence in the House. The people were irritated and suffering. Every measure he proposed was resisted by the intrigues of his rivals. But he set to work resolutely to meet the crisis. As Carlyle insists, Pitt's eye was ever on America. He saw the need of sending out to Canada something more than the "two miserable battalions," which he had formerly denounced. He now adopted an expedient which was a stroke of genius, inasmuch as it gave new blood to the British army, whilst it pacified and employed the angry blood in the Scotch Highlands. Two battalions of Highlanders—each one thousand strong—were at once enrolled, and the command given to chiefs of their own clans. His design was to recover Cape Breton and Quebec and drive the French from Canada. Stringent orders were sent to the naval and military commanders across the Atlantic to make every effort to strengthen the army and the fleet. Eight battalions were sent to America. Fleets were also ordered to the West Indies, to the Mediterranean, and to India. Votes for the year 1757 were for £8,355,320: 55,000 men for the navy; 45,000 for the army.

One of the first difficulties was the fate of the unfortunate Admiral Byng, in which the conduct of Pitt must be pronounced to be wise, generous, and bold. After Byng's ignominious retreat before the French fleet, leaving Minorca to its fate, the rage

and shame of the nation had forced Fox and Newcastle
to order the Admiral home for court-martial. He was
not tried until six months after his return. The court
consisted of four admirals and nine captains. By
the twelfth article of war every seaman who, *through
cowardice, negligence, or disaffection*, should not do his
utmost to take or destroy an enemy's ship with
which he was engaged shall suffer death. The four
admirals and the nine captains heard evidence and
the defence, and then acquitted Byng of cowardice
and of disaffection; but they unanimously found him
guilty of not *having done his utmost*, and accordingly
condemned him to be shot. They added a recommendation to mercy, on the ground that his offence
was "an error of judgment."

Thereupon violent agitation arose in the public,
and debates in Parliament. The King, and apparently
officers in both services, as well as the general public,
felt that Byng had brought disgrace upon the navy by
a fatal act of weakness. Politicians hoped that the
recommendation to mercy would prevail; but nearly
all of them hesitated to urge it on the King. Fox,
who was Leader of the House when Byng was recalled,
tried to throw the *onus* on Pitt. Stern disciplinarian
as he ever was, Pitt affirmed in Parliament that he
desired mercy to be shown. He went to the King, and
told him that the House of Commons desired a pardon.
The King cut him short by saying, "You have taught
me to look elsewhere than to the Commons for the
sense of my subjects!" It was stated in the House
that Captain Keppel, one of the court, had doubts
about the sentence. Pitt procured a respite from the

King. He carried a Bill to release the members of the
court-martial from their oath of secrecy (by 153
against 23).[1] The Bill went to the House of Lords,
where each member of the court-martial was separately
cross-examined by Lord Hardwicke and Lord Mansfield, the greatest living lawyers, who asked each
officer if he thought the sentence *unjust*. They all
answered in the negative. Thereupon the Lords
threw out the Bill, and left Byng to his fate. He was
shot on the 14th March 1757, having shown the utmost
intrepidity and dignity of bearing.

On this famous incident, so ill-understood even now,
one may observe :—

1. That Byng was not executed *in haste* : he was
shot nine months after his arrest, and three months
after his trial, after long debates in both Houses and
frequent respites.

2. He was not executed simply from popular clamour,
for the House of Lords were his worst opponents ; and
two of the greatest lawyers who ever sat there were
his severest judges.

3. The Court, the politicians, and the nation were
all agreed that Byng had lowered his country's flag,
and merited severe punishment—degradation, if not
death. The Article left no alternative but death.

4. The cooler minds saw that the admiral's offence

---

[1] It was on the debate of this Bill that Pitt said : "May I fall
when I refuse pity to such a suit as Mr. Keppel's, justifying a man
who lies under captivity and the shadow of death ! I thank God I
feel something more than popularity—I feel justice !" Lord Temple,
at the head of the Admiralty, had refused to sign the death-warrant
until its legality was referred to the judges. This was done. It was
pronounced to be legal.

was fatal error of judgment rather than "negligence," and they were willing to give him the benefit of the doubt.

5. Pitt and Temple fairly did their best to save his life at the risk of facing the anger of the King, the contempt of the people, and the intrigues of political rivals.

Pitt now accomplished what was perhaps the most conspicuous *volte-face* in the whole of his many-sided career. He who for twenty years had stormed against German entanglements and subsidies to foreign sovereigns, he who had won fame as a youth by sneering at Hanover and the King, now opened his own ministry to George II. by advising an alliance with Frederick of Prussia, and by proposing a vote of £200,000 for the war. It must be admitted that the change was strong, for Pitt had condemned this very treaty with Frederick only the year before; and so far as his policy can be said to have regular principle, it was to establish British ascendency at sea, and across the ocean, but not to meddle in the centre of Europe. The critics were ready to sneer. Fox was equal to the occasion and to himself, when he reminded Pitt of his famous trope that "the German measures would be a millstone round the neck of the minister," and he could but hope this German measure would prove to be an ornament round the neck of the present minister.

This was a very pretty bit of parliamentary satire. But the case was now changed; the men were different; and the purpose was not the same. Pitt cared little for rigid consistency, for unchangeable alliances and eternal enmities. He would not have been a great statesman if he did. He saw that he had been wrong in opposing the alliance with Frederick, that he had not understood the man. He saw it, and he frankly admitted it. To prevent Prussia being crushed by the gigantic confederacy of five Powers was a very different thing from assisting Maria Theresa to regain her ancestral dominions. Lastly, to protect Hanover from being absorbed by France, because the Elector of Hanover was King of England, was a very different thing from flinging away English blood and treasure to promote the ambition and second the quarrels of the Elector of Hanover. Pitt's policy, as he clearly showed, was this :—he would not sacrifice British interests for Hanoverian objects, but he would not let Hanover be sacrificed solely by reason of its connection with England. This was a perfectly intelligible policy ; and it was a sound policy. Pitt's change of front was startling ; but it has an adequate defence.

When Pitt was at last admitted to the closet of his ungracious King, he behaved with ostentatious, perhaps preposterous, humility ; would not be seated in the royal presence ; and, when unable to stand for his gout, would address his sovereign kneeling on a stool. Carlyle will have it that Pitt "had some reverence for George." Not for the man, one thinks ; but Pitt, in his imaginative and tragedy-king vein, seems to have felt the visible presence of his Sacred Majesty as a sort of consecration of his own power. His Sacred Majesty, at any rate at first, showed small reverence for the odious minister who forced himself on his King, and grumbled at the debating speeches he was required to listen to from his counsellor. Queen Victoria, it is whispered, complained that Mr. Gladstone "talked to her as if she were a public meeting." Pitt, we may be sure, talked to George as he had talked to the ministry of Walpole or Granville. George said Pitt was tedious and pompous, and had never read books on International Law. He was "alternately harsh and subservient to his sovereign," they said. As to Temple, —who was free and easy, treated the King as if he were Newcastle or Granville, and dared to say that Byng had merely shown the same prudence as George had shown at Oudenarde—the King found him unbearable. He said, "Now ministers are king."

Cumberland, who was to command the army sent to Germany, almost stipulated that Pitt should be dismissed before he sailed. Newcastle, who still controlled a great party in the Commons, and Fox, who was thirsting for place, carried on a set of incessant intrigues, which fill the *Memoirs* and make them as amusing as any romance. George at last saw an opportunity to strike his blow. Temple was summarily dismissed from the Admiralty. Pitt refused to resign. The King sent for his seals and those of Mr. Legge, the Chancellor of the Exchequer. Pitt's friends in the government followed him and resigned.

For eleven weeks the game of ministerial combinations went on with as many surprises and changes as any in the *Comedy of Errors* or the *Fourberies de Scapin*. The public excitement was intense. The Stocks fell. The City voted Pitt its freedom in a costly casket. The other great towns followed suit. Walpole says— "for some weeks it rained gold boxes." The agitation was almost like that which carried the Reform Bill of 1832. Endless combinations of Peers and Commoners were tried and torn up in a day. In the meantime Parliament was sitting; a war was being waged at sea and land; there was no government; the King, the Duke of Cumberland, the Prince of Wales and his mother—all had their own partisans pulling different ways. In the House, an inquiry was being forced on, to fix the responsibility for the loss of Minorca and other disasters. If Pitt had used all his fire, it is thought he might have crushed for ever both Newcastle and Fox.

The amazing and amusing result of all such serio-comedy was this. Instead of crushing Newcastle and Fox, who had just driven him from power, instead of defying the King, who had rudely dismissed him, Pitt became his absolute First Minister, and that in coalition with Newcastle, with Fox, and even with that "execrable minister," Carteret-Granville. The wonderful *peripeteia* has been told by Macaulay with such truth and such conciseness, that it is well to borrow his account. Pitt, he says, had found by experience that he could not stand alone. Without rank, without fortune, without borough interest, hated by the King, hated by the aristocracy, he was still a person of the first importance in the state. He had formed a ministry, had excluded his chief rivals from it—these the most powerful Whig Peer and the ablest debater in the Commons.

He now found that he had gone too far. He had the people, but no majority in the people's House. Newcastle had wealth, rank, parliamentary influence, prestige, long practice in intrigue. Fox in oratorical power was only inferior to Pitt, and in adroit debating even his superior. The King preferred Newcastle; Cumberland held by Fox; the public clamoured for Pitt. Newcastle had been turned out by the public indignation. Pitt had been turned out by want of parliamentary backing. Newcastle wanted patronage more than power. Fox wanted money more than power. Pitt wanted nothing but power, and refused to share it with Newcastle or with Fox. Newcastle, Fox, or Pitt each could turn out the other two. Neither could maintain a government alone. United they would be irresistible. Pitt, Fox, and Newcastle's nominees need fear no opposition in the House. The Duke could answer for the army of place-hunters and the benevolent neutrality of the magnates. Pitt could rouse the cities, the services, and the nation to a white heat of enthusiasm. In face of such a coalition, the King, the royalties, and the factions could do nothing.

After infinite negotiations and shuffling of the cards, in which Lord Chesterfield, Lord Hardwicke, and Lord Mansfield played important parts, and Pitt showed firmness and dignity, a combination was secured whereby Pitt gained everything he desired. He himself became Secretary of State, Leader of the House of Commons, and undoubted First Minister. The Duke was one of the Commissioners at the Treasury along with George Grenville, where he could continue to job and patronise to his heart's content. Fox was kicked downstairs from cabinet rank into the Pay Office, where he was content to make a vast fortune by illicit perquisites. Legge returned to the Exchequer, and Temple returned as Privy Seal.

Granville, a drunkard and a wreck, remained President of the Council. On the face of it, this might seem to be the old ministry of Newcastle, Fox, and Pitt. In truth, it was nothing of the kind. It was a ministry in which Pitt was absolute master; the rest were ciphers. Newcastle retained jobbery without power or dignity. Fox obtained money without power or rank. Both were practically degraded. Pitt had placed his friends, George Grenville, James Grenville, Temple, and Legge, where he wanted them. He had the sole control. He now broke with the pocket-borough system, having sat during twenty years for seats in the gift of his own family or of the Pelhams. He now had himself elected for the city of Bath, where indeed he had to pass many weary months as an invalid. The King was checkmated. Parliament became obsequious and silent; and Pitt, freed from the solicitations of obscure place-hunters and the worry of a strong opposition, was able to devote his whole soul to the nation. This ministry, for now it was really Pitt's ministry, in four years won more temporary glory and effected more permanent results than any English ministry [1] within the same time.

Pitt, now in sole control at the helm of state, devoted himself with intense ardour to all the details of administration, so far as concerned military and naval affairs, and foreign policy. In these he was all that Frederick was in Prussia, or Napoleon was as

[1] Lord Waldegrave, who went to Kensington to watch the new ministers present themselves to the King, says Pitt and his friends were decent and sensible: neither insolent nor awkward. The Duke and his party showed such fear and shame that made them objects of pity.

Emperor. He spared no labour; nothing was too small for his attention. His orders were exact, clear, peremptory; his dispatches lucid expositions of definite policies. The special characteristic of his rule lay in the choice of fit men to lead an expedition, to devise a plan of strategy, or to conduct a negotiation. He utterly discarded seniority as a ground of promotion. He would pick out for service new men, usually young, often unknown men. He would trust them with full powers, and took personal care to give them resources adequate for each task. It was his wonderful power of judging men, of measuring the needs of each undertaking beforehand, of insisting on rapidity and punctuality, of following up each blow by another, that secured such dazzling results in action. Civilian as he was, Pitt filled each man he employed with that patriotic passion which Frederick, Nelson, and Napoleon infused into their officers and men. It was said—No one ever left Pitt's cabinet without feeling himself a braver man.

Though he was "constitutional minister" in a parliamentary government, Pitt soon became as peremptory and despotic as Frederick or Napoleon himself. Many are the tales of his dictatorial ways. He often bearded the King, as when George, in a rage at his son's signing the surrender of Kloster-Zeven, cried out, "I gave him no orders to treat!" "No, Sir," said Pitt, "but you gave him very full powers!" The story went that when the Duke of Newcastle hesitated to sign Treasury orders for army stores, Pitt sent word that he would have the Duke impeached. When a general complained that he could not obtain the

supplies he needed, Pitt sent round to each Board royal
commands to have these demands immediately satisfied.   Lord Anson had been forced on Pitt as head of
the Admiralty by the King and Lord Hardwicke,
Anson's father-in-law.   Pitt compelled the Naval Commissioners to countersign his own dispatches, which
he would not allow them to read.   So Lord Temple
declared, and that he actually sent out fleets with
sealed orders without suffering the Board of Admiralty,
which supplied and commissioned them, to know
whither they were sent.

From the first Pitt conceived a set of grand schemes.
He found his country at war with France, and the
great Coalition of Sovereigns ready to crush Prussia
and Hanover.   He decided to save both ; and, in order
to create a diversion to the west, he prepared an
invasion of France in the Bay of Biscay.   At the
same time he arranged to supply Frederick with men
and money without stint.   He sent strong reinforcements to the East Indies to second the efforts of the
Company, where the genius of Clive was about to
found an Empire.   The French ports, both on the
Atlantic and in the Mediterranean, were to be watched
and blockaded, whilst the French fleets were to be
driven from the seas.   Above all, the French settlement in Canada was to be annexed, and the British
dominion secured in the valleys of the St. Lawrence
and of the Mississippi and Ohio.   These mighty results,
in distant lands and in four different continents, were
all effected within a few years by one who was neither
Sovereign nor Conqueror, but a decrepit civilian who
only left St. James's Square for Hayes or the waters

of Bath, who never "set a squadron in the field," but
who "organised victory," as was said of Carnot, by
his true and far-reaching vision, by insight into human
capacities, by fiery energy, and by infusing into a
nation his own heroic soul.

It must be admitted that the first expeditions on
the Continent were anything but successful. The
Duke of Cumberland was defeated in Germany, and
made a pitiable surrender, which his father repudiated,
disowning his son with passion. Pitt, whom the Duke
had striven to degrade, generously stood by the fallen
commander, and enabled him to escape further punishment by resigning his office and retiring into civil life.
He then induced George to appoint Prince Ferdinand
of Brunswick commander of an army of 30,000 Hanoverians, who before long drove the French from the
Electorate and protected Frederick on that side. This
at last overcame the ill-will of King George ; for Pitt
was now himself become "a Hanover-troop minister,"
indeed under quite altered circumstances. "Give me
your confidence, Sire," said the minister, "and I will
deserve it." "Deserve my confidence, Sir," said the
King in turn, "and you shall have it." The King,
who wanted neither sense nor a rough wit, had the
best of the altercation. At last he saw that Pitt deserved his confidence, and he henceforth steadily gave it.

The expeditions against the coast of France did not
effect very much. A very powerful fleet was de-
spatched to Rochefort, with sealed orders to seize
that fort. A large army was placed on board, and
great preparations for a landing were made. The
whole French coast was alarmed, and the nation

astonished. Such secrecy was observed as to the objective of attack that Lord Anson, at the head of the Admiralty, was not allowed to know their destination. He told Pitt that it was impossible to comply with his orders for the ships and their equipment. Pitt replied that he would have Anson impeached if they were not ready at the time ordered. In result, the expedition was mismanaged and nothing effective was done. A fresh expedition was organised, which landed and attacked St. Malo, but with small results. A third expedition destroyed the forts at Cherbourg, capturing cannon and colours and ammunition. A fourth expedition against St. Malo met with a disastrous repulse, with the loss of a thousand men in killed, wounded, and prisoners.

These repeated expeditions to attack French seaports have been severely criticised as the weakest parts of Pitt's schemes, and even as preposterous follies. They were indeed very costly demonstrations. Fox said "it was breaking windows with guineas." King George said, "You may brag of taking their guns: they will brag that they drove you away!" Lord George Sackville refused to command the last expedition, and said he "wanted no more buccaneering." From Pitt's point of view of defeating the French, there is something to be said to the contrary. Of the four expeditions, the last only had ended in repulse and defeat. The first three had been effected absolutely without loss in ships or men; and if they had brought no permanent advantage, they had inflicted on the enemy humiliation and alarm. Pitt well remembered the confusion and paralysis caused in England at the panic of a French expedition being about to invade our shores. He no doubt counted on the effect in France of four actual descents on French soil, and the attack and capture of their forts and fortresses. He could not expect to retain any footing on the territory of France. But he amply secured his main objects —to make the Continent feel the ascendency of Britain at sea, and to draw off French forces from Germany to the defence of their western seaboard. Frederick of Prussia and Ferdinand of Brunswick admitted that this had been accomplished. Wanton and idle in themselves, these costly attacks on the French ports must be judged as part of the central scheme of Pitt's policy. This now was: to destroy the vast colonial settlements in Asia, Africa, and America which France had been building up for a generation, and to plant on their ruins a still vaster British Empire. And to secure this end it was essential to crush the French naval power, and to paralyse the naval bases of the French fleets.

Another remarkable scheme of Pitt's, to aid in the war on France, was his secret proposal to Spain in 1757 to cede Gibraltar, which for fifty years had been in British possession, on condition of Spain joining the war against France, and enabling Britain to recover Minorca from the French. Pitt induced the King and his cabinet to join in this momentous offer, taking great pains with a long dispatch he wrote himself in three days to present to the Spanish Court every argument which might operate on their minds. The Spanish Court declined to entertain the proposal, having no taste for a war with France, however great their eagerness to recover their historic fort. Gibraltar accordingly has flown the Union Jack for exactly two hundred years, with all the consequences that we know. How different many things would have been if Spain had listened to Pitt's proposal! That it should have been made by such a man at such a time may serve to illustrate the range of his ideas, and the ascendency he had now acquired over the King and his advisers.

"The warfare of 1758 was waged through all the four quarters of the globe," says Earl Stanhope, in the grand manner of his great kinsman himself. Wherever France had laid the foundations of Empire,—in India, in Africa, in America,—there Pitt, not content with bombarding her western ports, and driving her armies out of Hanover, continued to assail her by a British fleet and constant expeditions. The French under Colbert had wrung from the Portuguese and the Dutch the valuable colony of Senegal, stretching for five hundred miles on the West Coast of Africa from Cape Blanco to the Gambia. They held Fort Louis on the mouth of the Senegal, and fortified the island of Goree, which commanded the Gambia. A Quaker merchant having proposed to Pitt an expedition to annex the settlement, which this "passive resister," with an eye to the main chance, assured him could be effected "without bloodshed," he straightway dispatched a fleet with about one thousand marines and regular troops—in what would now be called "a peaceful mission of commerce." The French forces were over-powered; and for some years Senegal remained under the British flag.

This ministry of Pitt marks also the foundation of the British Empire in India, which is usually dated from the victory of Plassey in 1757 over the Nabob of Bengal and that of Wandewash in 1761 over the French Lally. But these events belong to the life of Clive or of Sir Eyre Coote, not to that of Chatham; and they need not be recorded here except in outline. The record of daring, of fraud, of rapacity, of genius and heroism by which that wonderful dominion was rapidly achieved come only in an incidental way into the career of Chatham. When he first entered into power in England, the East India Company were still struggling to hold their ground against the French, and had merely an insecure foothold in Madras and Calcutta. Clive was restoring their fortunes and making his own by marvellous feats of audacity, vigour, and unscrupulous genius both for policy and war. He saved to the Company Madras and the Carnatic; he was the real founder of Calcutta; he secured Bengal. He struck right and left at the French settlements or the Dutch, and made the Hoogly a British river. The British then turned upon the French settlement, and by the sword of Sir Eyre Coote at Wandewash, the defeat of the brave Lally Tollendal, and the capture of Pondicherry, finally extinguished the prospects of a French empire in Hindustan. Those momentous four years from 1757 to 1761 had changed the whole future of the Indian Peninsula. But the home government had no great share in the work, beyond supporting the Company with able soldiers and a small fleet. It was the star of Pitt rather than his genius which made his ministry coincide with the birth of that Raj which has now made the King of England Emperor of Hindustan. The deeds by which it was founded cannot be set down except indirectly to increase his glory or to burden his last account at the Judgment-Seat of human history.

Pitt most ardently supported the Company and its officers in their struggles, as his zealous temper in part inspired their courage. In the famous speech he made in the Parliament of December 1757, reported only in fragments by Horace Walpole, we are told how he "burst out into an Eastern panegyric. There he found Watson, Pococke, and Clive :—what astonishing success had Watson had with only three ships, which had been laid up for some time on land ! He did not stay to careen this, and condemn that, but at once sailed into the body of the Ganges. He was supported by Clive, that man not born for a desk ; *that heaven-born General*, whose magnanimity, resolution, determination, and execution would charm a King of Prussia, and whose presence of mind astonished the Indies !" We may feel sure that these were not Pitt's exact words. But we can see the meaning, and can understand how the thrill of them would pass across the ocean to Bengal and the Carnatic.

With the conquest of Canada and the establishment of the British name in the valley of the Mississippi it was far otherwise. Here the design, the choice of men, the preparation of the armaments both by sea and land was the work of Pitt, and almost solely his direct and personal work. This is the part of his policy which produced the greatest and most abiding effects

upon the face of the world.   He saw from the first the
vast possibilities in the American Continent.   He saw
that the only serious rivals to be feared were France
or Spain, both powers having fleets and strong places
on the other side of the Atlantic.   With a view of
detaching Spain from France, Pitt had sent friendly
overtures to Spain coupled with the dazzling bribe of
the conditional cession of Gibraltar in exchange for
Minorca.   He now determined to assail the French
possessions in America on all sides at once.   He grasped
the essential condition of success, and saw the cause of
the late disasters which had befallen his first attempts
and those of his predecessors.   It was necessary to
send an overpowering force, and at the same time by
our superior sea-power to intercept all reinforcements
from Europe.   This had failed in the year 1757.   Pitt
now prepared a still larger force, which was to be
backed up with several fleets.   He was bent on nothing
short of driving the French flag from the whole North
American continent.

The preparations for the eventful year 1758 were
on a formidable scale, which might make Walpole turn
in his grave.   Supplies were voted for about ten
millions and a half.   £1,861,000 was devoted to
foreign subsidies.   There were to be 60,000 seamen
and 86,500 land forces, or, including the Irish service,
100,000 men.   An immense fleet of forty-one ships
under Admiral Boscawen was sent out in February to
reinforce the fleet at Halifax.   To cut off reinforcements from France, Spain, or the Mediterranean, Lord
Hawke with seven ships was sent to blockade the
French ports; and Osborne with fifteen ships was sent

to cruise along the coast of Spain, and cut off any fleet from the Spanish or Mediterranean ports. Young, daring, and ambitious soldiers were chosen for important commands: Wolfe, Lord Howe, Amherst, Forbes, men of the stamp of Clive, who were promoted over all their seniors in rank. Pitt devised three separate expeditions, two directed against Canada, one into the Mississippi valley; and he furnished all three with ample forces, elaborate instructions, and peremptory orders. The whole was based on exhaustive study of the local conditions and the strategical problems.

The first expedition was directed against Louisburg in the island of Cape Breton, and was the most important of all. Louisburg was the most valuable port that France possessed on the American continent. It commanded the entrance to the Gulf of St. Lawrence. The fleet which made this its base could effectually close the whole length of the River St. Lawrence and its valley, and prevent it from receiving succour by sea. Against that cardinal point in the defences of Canada, Admiral Boscawen and General Amherst were sent in June with a fleet of 150 sail and an army of nearly 12,000 men. The fortress was very strong and amply prepared for a siege. The invaders were far stronger in ships and in men, but were heavily impeded by bad weather. By the heroism of the young Wolfe and the audacity and resource of Boscawen's seamen, Louisburg fell in July, and with it the island of St. John's in the Gulf. The St. Lawrence was henceforth closed to France.

It is no part of the *Life* of Pitt to describe the opera-

tions of war achieved by the fleets and armies he
dispatched.   When the ships had sailed across the
Atlantic, the minister at home had no power to influence the issue.   The conquest of Canada, the cross-
ing of the Alleghanies and securing to Britain the
valley of the Ohio, belong to the history of England,
to the biographies of Wolfe, Amherst, Forbes, and
Washington, but only in general design concern the
biographer of Pitt.   The second expedition was aimed
at that long basin stretching northwards from Fort
William Henry at the foot of Lake George, through
Forts Ticonderoga and Crown Point to Lake Champlain, and thence by the Richelieu river to Sorel in
the valley of St. Lawrence, half-way between Montreal
and Quebec.   The force destined to strike this blow
consisted of some 15,000 troops, of whom 6000 were
British regulars, with more than a thousand lake boats.
They were commanded by General James Abercromby,
who owed his appointment more to political influence
than to his own energy or resource; but Pitt had
chosen as his lieutenant and real leader the young
and gallant Lord Howe, whom he himself called
"the complete model of military virtue."   Howe
was named by his men and his brother officers, as
by Wolfe himself, the best soldier in the British
army; and little doubt can exist that, had he lived
to lead the expedition, its immense strength and
equipment would have given it victory.   But on the
first day of landing from Lake George, in order to
approach Ticonderoga, Howe was killed in a skirmish,
possibly by a shot from his own men whilst he was
leading the attack.   Abercromby was incapable of

following up so adventurous an attack on a fort
defended by the brilliant Montcalm with 3600 good
men. After losing 2000 of his force, the feeble
Abercromby beat a retreat and was recalled home
amidst the bitter groans of the government and the
nation.

A partial, and not unimportant success, was won
by Bradstreet with a part of Abercromby's force.
Having persuaded that general to let him lead 3000
provincial troops to the westwards against Fort Oswego
on the Ontario Lake, he pushed across it and captured
Fort Frontenac, which stands at the north-eastern end
of Lake Ontario, whence the St. Lawrence river issues
to the sea. With the surrender of Fort Frontenac,
Bradstreet captured all the French ships on Lake
Ontario, which henceforward served as a British base.
By these simultaneous captures of Louisburg and
Frontenac, though separated by nearly one thousand
miles of waterway, the valley of the St. Lawrence
was closed to the French, both at its source in Lake
Ontario on the south-west, and on its outfall into
the Gulf on the north-east. And at the same time
the command of Lake Ontario brought the British
within measurable distance of the headwaters of
the Alleghany river whereon stood Fort Duquesne,
the spot where the defeat and repulse of Braddock
in 1755 had roused such just indignation and alarm.

The third expedition was to pass due west from
Pennsylvania, to cross the Alleghany Mountains and
to attack Fort Duquesne, which lies at the junction
of several rivers all flowing into the Ohio, and is
situated about three hundred miles from the Atlantic

seaboard. This force consisted of 1400 Highlanders and about 5000 or 6000 Colonials. It had a very arduous task, owing to the approach of winter and the unknown road through virgin forests and a lofty mountain range. It was commanded by General Forbes, a soldier of great energy and prudence, having as his second, Colonel George Washington, whose splendid conduct in the rout of Braddock three years before had raised him to the command of the Colonial troops. Forbes started from Philadelphia in July; but his excessive caution in advancing by stages from one fortified post to another, the mountainous route, and the bad weather, delayed him so that he did not reach Fort Duquesne until the end of November. He found it evacuated by the French and the fortifications blown up. Their force was wholly incapable of resisting Forbes's army ; and the capture of Frontenac by Bradstreet had stopped the supplies which were to reach them by way of the Northern Lakes. Fort Duquesne being destroyed, Forbes, stricken as he was with mortal disease, planted a new fort on this most dominant spot, to which he gave the name of Pitt. He wrote to Pitt (27th November): "I have used the freedom of giving your name to Fort Duquesne, as I hope it was in some measure the being actuated by your spirits that now makes us masters of the place."

Pitt in his reply (of 23rd January 1759) praises in fitting terms the well-concerted plan, the prudence, judgment, and resolution which has won this success "of the highest importance." He presses on the general the need of using every effort to retain control of the Ohio valley, to cultivate the loyal co-operation and union of the Colonists, and to conciliate and form alliances with the Indian tribes. The genius of Pitt at once descried the value of this new possession. Pittsburg stands on the junction of the Alleghany and the Monongahela rivers with the grand Ohio ; and with its dependencies it has to-day a population of quite half a million. It is one of the great industrial centres, and the point of junction of immense lines of railroad. Neither Pitt nor Washington, nor any man in that century, could possibly have foreseen that the new settlement was to grow into the greatest iron and coal centre of the world, as little as they could have imagined how a penniless Scotch lad would one day build up from out its lurid furnaces a colossal business, of which the profits were ultimately to spread across America and Britain the means of learning and culture.[1] How few of all the toilers in those mines and steel-yards, how few of all those citizens or tourists who pass through the Iron City towards the Northern Lakes or the Western plains, remember how the name of Pittsburg recalls the fact that Pitt and Washington, separated as they were by 3000 miles of ocean, combined in planting that dominant stronghold whence the Far West of the continent was ultimately secured to their common race !

But an achievement far more brilliant in itself, and

---

[1] Andrew Carnegie, born at Dunfermline, and now of New York and Skibo Castle, developed at Pittsburg the immense steel-works, and thence accumulated the vast fortune which he has since devoted to the cause of public education.

even more momentous in its issue on the future of
the British Empire, was now undertaken by the
aspiring genius of Pitt.   It was nothing less than
the conquest of Canada from the French, who had
been in complete occupation of that vast district for
two centuries.   The central expedition was to ascend
the St. Lawrence river and to attack the cities of
Quebec and Montreal.   But this was to be supported
by three other lines of attack : one from the Lakes
George and Champlain to the St. Lawrence ; the
second from Fort Niagara on Lake Ontario to reach
the source of the St. Lawrence river ; the third from
Pittsburg to Lake Erie.   This vast area of combined
operations, extending over an extent of six hundred
or seven hundred miles through a wild country with
virgin forests and unbridged rivers, could hardly be
a complete success even in the most perfect conditions
of modern war.   The strategic conception was gigantic
and practically beyond the resources of the age.   No
one of the three supporting movements quite effected
its object or reached the goal—which was the St.
Lawrence valley—in time.   But important results
were obtained by all three ; and they greatly contributed to the ultimate triumph.

The main task was entrusted to the youthful
General James Wolfe—who, though then but thirty-
two, had seen sixteen years of active service in war,
and had fought in great and desperate battles in
Germany, in France, and in America.   At the age
of twenty-one he had been publicly thanked by his
commander.   At twenty-two he had won his rank of
Colonel.   If he had been in command at Rochefort,

it was believed the attack would have succeeded. The
conquest of Cape Breton was mainly his work. This
was the youthful hero—the Nelson of the Army he
has been called—whom Pitt selected to lead the
arduous task of the conquest of Canada.

The young general was put in command of an army
of some 8600 excellent soldiers, supported by a fleet
which numbered in all nearly fifty sail. They were
opposed by the gallant Montcalm, who had more than
15,000 men, mostly native levies, with a strong and
skilful contingent of Indians. The story of that
amazing victory belongs rather to the history of
England and of the British Empire than to the *Life* of
Pitt. What Englishman does not know that stirring
and pathetic epic? How, for eleven weeks, the
British force sought to pierce some joint in the vast
defences that Montcalm had spread round Quebec—
how the fortress, towering like another Gibraltar
above the rushing tide of the St. Lawrence, seemed
to defy the attacks, whilst Montcalm, with an army
nearly double that of Wolfe, lay entrenched below its
ramparts—how Wolfe himself, racked with disease,
anxiety, and fever, having exhausted every device,
and having lost a tenth of his whole command, wrote
home to Pitt a dispatch full of ominous doubts, but
ending with the promise of one last effort—how, by a
kind of heroic intuition, he put his whole force on
barges at night and silently stole past the sleeping
enemy, till he reached the other side of the mighty
fortress—how in the darkness a few thousand Highlanders and Grenadiers scaled the precipitous crags
which rise three hundred feet from the water's edge

and dragged up there a single cannon—how in the
morning the French general to his amazement found
the British army drawn up in line of battle on the
height which he had considered unscaleable, and had
given no adequate guard—how a desperate battle took
place under the walls of the citadel—short, sharp,
and decisive, a battle wherein the first and second
generals in command on both sides fell—how Wolfe
was thrice wounded and died in the very arms of
victory within a few yards of his noble opponent—
how the memory of both is enshrined in one common
monument, dear to Briton as to Frank—how this
sudden, unhoped for, almost impossible triumph sent a
thrill through the whole British race, and practically
decided the mighty issue—the transfer of the Northern
half of the American continent from the French to the
English Crown. It is a household word with the
English race ; nor need the circumstances be again
rehearsed in the *Life* of Pitt. The hand that did the
deed was the hand of Wolfe. But the voice that
bade it to be done—the eye that saw its future possibilities—the brain which conceived it, was the voice,
the eye, the brain of Pitt.

The joy of the nation, passing from the depths of
anxiety to the extravagance of triumph, but darkened
by the loss of the young leader, was well painted
in the famous passage of Walpole's *Memoirs*. "The
incidents of dramatic fiction could not be conducted
with more address to lead an audience from despon-
dency to sudden exultation, than accident prepared
to excite the passions of a whole people. They de-
spaired—they triumphed—and they wept—for Wolfe

had fallen in the hour of victory! Joy, grief, curiosity, astonishment, were painted in every countenance; the more they inquired, the higher their admiration rose. Not an incident but was heroic and affecting!" The popular instinct coupled the names of Pitt and Wolfe as the authors of this astonishing success, which even inspired the gentle soul of Cowper to celebrate them both together in his *Task*—a passage wherein patriotism has almost extinguished poetry.

The capture of Quebec, after a series of hazards and vicissitudes as striking as any in the history of war, was almost followed by its recapture. The French recovered from their panic, and severely defeated the British garrison, who were only saved by the timely arrival of a few ships of war. The French then withdrew up the St. Lawrence for a last stand at Montreal. From East, West, and South, three British forces were now concentrated on the city—one from the St. Lawrence, one from Lake Champlain, and one from Lake Ontario—the three concentric armies as originally designed by Pitt, and now amounting to 17,000 men. Slowly, but surely, in spite of extraordinary difficulties from virgin forests, rapids, and rocks, the three British armaments met at Montreal. Nothing remained to the gallant Frenchmen but unconditional surrender. On September 8, 1760, Canada and all its dependencies passed to the British Crown. French soldiers and sailors were sent back to France in British ships. Free exercise of religion, their local French law, and their property, were guaranteed to all Canadians and to all Frenchmen who chose to remain.

Thus by a few sudden strokes, half a continent passed over to Great Britain. And for one hundred and forty years the vast wilderness north of the St. Lawrence and the Great Lakes, far away to the Pacific, has been steadily filling up with British settlers, and forming a vigorous element in the British Empire. But, socially and politically, the foundation of Fort Pitt, and the expulsion of the French from the valleys of the Ohio and the Mississippi, was an even more momentous achievement. A few years before 1760, the French had claimed for their own sphere of influence the whole American continent north of the St. Lawrence and west of the Ohio. They mainly controlled the native Indian tribes, and they held military posts along the valleys of the St. Lawrence and of the Mississippi. This dominion was far too vast for France in the age of Louis XV. to maintain or to people. From the mouths of the Mississippi to Cape Breton, the key of the St. Lawrence, is a distance of more than two thousand miles. The claim was not based on population, or any real power. But it had an imposing show, and it rested on a skilfully constructed network of forts. Had the claim been made good, more than half the American continent would have remained under the French flag, would have maintained the language, laws, and political system of France.

Mr. J. R. Green, the Historian of the English People, tells us that "with the triumph of Wolfe, the history of the United States began,"—"Pitt laid the foundation of the great Republic of the West." "Really a considerable Fact in the History of the

World," says Carlyle—"Fact principally due to Pitt."
This is no place to moralise over the fierce rivalry
of races and the selfish ambition of statesmen. The
historical facts are our immediate concern. And no
years in modern history are more pregnant with
incalculable issues than those closing years of the
reign of George II., wherein it was finally decided that
the English language, common law, literature, and
blood, should be settled on the continent of America
from the Atlantic to the Pacific, from the Arctic
Ocean to the Gulf of Mexico. The Colonies felt the
great future that was now opened to them with a
clear vision which was hardly possible in Europe.
The pulpits of New England resounded with thanks-
giving, and a young preacher at Boston declared that,
with the continued blessing of Heaven, the Colonies
"will become, in another century or two, a mighty
empire"—"not independent of the mother country,"
he added. Such are the forecasts of man!

Full of visions of a transoceanic Empire to be,
Pitt relentlessly pursued his scheme to crush the
maritime power of France and of Spain, the only two
powers which then had to be considered at sea. He
saw clearly, as Captain Mahan has lucidly shown,
that, if France had been driven from America and
from India, and Spain had been checked in the West
Indies, it had been effected by the naval ascendency
of Britain. And as to Pitt and to the men of his
age colonies meant exclusive Commerce, and the
monopoly of Trade meant wealth, and commercial
wealth meant national strength, Pitt passionately
aimed at barring the rivals of his country from found-

ing colonial possessions or pushing a transoceanic
trade. He could nurse no illusion as to the possibility
of holding any French territory in Europe. But he
designed to crush any French settlement in any part of
the world; and he thoroughly understood that France
would be exhausted in the effort to retain any transmarine possession; whilst, by supporting Frederick of
Prussia, he caused her to drain herself in continental
wars.

These schemes were perfectly intelligible and consistently followed; and whatever we think of their
justice or wisdom, they were designed by a true
master of statecraft. The conquest of French colonies
on the West Coast of Africa was followed by the
capture of Guadeloupe and Marie Galante, and of some
small islands in the West Indies. The French were
now roused to make reprisals by a home-thrust on
their enemy, and the Duc de Choiseul boldly resolved
on a fresh invasion of England. Great preparations
were made at all ports; transports were collected;
ships of the line equipped; and troops assembled at
various points. They supposed that, as large fleets
and armies had been dispatched by Pitt to various
parts of the world, a descent on the English coast
might be effected. They did not rightly estimate the
difference between a Pitt and a Newcastle. In 1756
England had looked forward with alarm to a French
invasion. In 1759 it was treated with scorn.

The English minister calmly awaited the attack
without weakening his forces abroad. He proudly
reminded the Spanish government, which was being
solicited by France as an ally, that the King's regular

forces *in these islands* amounted to more than 40,000 men, that thirty-five ships of the line, besides frigates, were manned and equipped for *home service*. Over and above this, the militia was called out in full; bounties were offered to volunteer seamen and landsmen. Large sums in aid of parliamentary supplies were subscribed by London and the principal cities. A squadron was stationed off Dunkirk to blockade the French in that port; and a more powerful fleet under Admiral Hawke blockaded Brest. Rodney bombarded the French transports preparing in Havre. Boscawen with fourteen ships watched the port of Toulon in the Mediterranean; and, when the French fleet had issued through the Straits of Gibraltar, he chased them and destroyed or took five ships off Cape Lagos, near the southern angle of Portugal; and he drove the remainder of the French ships into Cadiz, where they were blockaded.

The French scheme of invasion was still persisted in. A violent storm in October, driving away the blockading forces, enabled two of their fleets to set sail; one from Dunkirk, and one from Brest. The fleet that escaped from Dunkirk was driven round Scotland to Ireland, and finally was captured in the Irish Channel. The larger fleet from Brest was driven into Quiberon Bay, a most dangerous and rocky coast; where Hawke, by splendid seamanship and rare audacity, broke up the fleet of Conflans of twenty-one ships of the line, and practically annihilated the navy of France. The naval victory of Quiberon Bay, gained almost entirely by skill and daring in handling ships in a gale on a treacherous coast, at a loss in killed of not more than forty men, ranks with La Hogue and Trafalgar in the history of the British navy. For a generation France ceased to be a great Sea Power.

Not content with tearing from France her nascent dominion in India, her new colonies on the Senegal in Africa, some West Indian islands, and the whole of her vast territories on the North American continent, Pitt resolutely supported Frederick in his war with France and her allies, and gave him immense subsidies year by year, and no small forces on land. He declared "that America could be won in Germany"— meaning, no doubt, that if France was made a principal in the Seven Years' War to crush Prussia, and thus exhausted herself in the struggle, she would leave Canada and the Mississippi valley to be conquered by the British. Pitt, says Carlyle, was "King of England for four years," and proved himself to be Frederick's principal and almost his only help. "Blessing" is Carlyle's phrase; and, whether we accept that term or not, we may take the biographer's word for it that Frederick largely owed his salvation to Pitt's alliance, nor was he slow to acknowledge it.

The events of that long and bloody strife belong to the history of Europe and of Germany, rather than to the *Life* of Pitt. The part played in it by England was intermittent, subordinate, and to a great extent financial. In four years Frederick received from England £2,680,000 sterling in money. Six treaties of alliance were made in the same period. Pitt began by taking the Hanoverian army of the Elector into English pay. He supported George II., when the King repudiated the treaty of Kloster-Zeven made by his son, which had opened Hanover to the French, and exposed Prussia on her north-western frontier. He then put the Hanoverian forces into the command of Prince Ferdinand of Brunswick, one of Frederick's best generals; and he placed a strong British contingent under the Prince's orders. At the battle of Minden, on the Weser, Ferdinand with inferior numbers inflicted a great defeat on the French. The English infantry and artillery contributed to the success in no small degree, and the enemy would have been utterly routed had it not been for the disloyal refusal of Lord George Sackville, the commander of the British cavalry, to obey the orders of the chief of whom he was jealous. Sackville was tried by court-martial, dismissed from the army, and was never forgiven by the King or by Pitt. The minister indeed gave the heartiest support to the German Prince, and placed his victory on a par with that of Hawke. The condition of France, as Voltaire says, was now disastrous: her armies beaten—her navy destroyed—her public credit bankrupt.

These tremendous efforts of Great Britain in four different continents had not been accomplished without a lavish sacrifice of ships, material, and money. When Pitt opened the session of 1758, he made no attempt to disguise the cost and the difficulties of the situation. He seemed to glory in his lavish estimates —"heaps of millions," he said, "must be raised." In that year £10,486,457 was voted; 60,000 seamen and 86,500 land forces, and 14,000 for Ireland. For the year 1759, £12,761,310 was voted. For the year 1760, £15,503,563 was voted, with an army of 100,000

men, and also 20,000 militia. The year 1760 was
the crowning moment of Pitt's war ministry. Madras
was added to Calcutta; Canada and the Ohio valley
were cleared of the French; four West Indian islands
had been captured, and the Senegal colony in Africa.
The French ports in the Bay of Biscay and in the
Mediterranean had been continuously blockaded, and
the navy of France had been annihilated. Lagos,
Quebec, Minden, Quiberon Bay, were decisive victories.
And twenty thousand British troops were fighting in
Germany in support of the King of Prussia. The
instinct of the nation justly attributed these rapid
triumphs to the inspiration of the statesman who
designed them. And our historian has confirmed this
view in words of hearty applause. "The ardour of his
soul had set the whole kingdom on fire. It inflamed
every soldier who dragged the cannon up the heights
of Quebec, and every sailor who boarded the French
ships among the rocks of Brittany. The minister,
before he had been long in office, had imparted to the
commanders whom he employed his own impetuous,
adventurous, and defying character."

In the same year a sudden event changed the whole
face of the political world, and reacted profoundly on
the career of Pitt. George II. died by a rupture of
the heart at Kensington, at the age of seventy-seven.
Having resisted the claims of Pitt for many years, and
having excluded him from many ministries, George
had at last given Pitt his entire confidence, and had
zealously seconded all his schemes. It was truly
said that Pitt had been King these four years. As
Mr. Goldwin Smith has happily expressed it: "Pitt's

ideal was to be a 'Patriot King'—only his King was
to be William—not George." But George II. was now
succeeded by George III., who had been trained from
boyhood by his mother to insist on being King himself, who was utterly out of sympathy with Pitt as
a man and with his policy as a statesman, and who
was under the influence of a feeble and ambitious
favourite. The first object of both was to undermine
and displace Pitt. From this day he ceases to wield
the power of England, and to be responsible for the
era of vacillating counsels and short-sighted measures
to which she was soon to be committed.

CHAPTER VII

FALL FROM POWER

FROM October 1760, when George II. died, until
October 1761, when Pitt resigned office, he was in
name First Minister, but he was not in power, he
was no longer "king." George III., destined to be
for many years the evil genius of our country, bred
up an Englishman, a Tory, and a bigot, had small
care for Hanover, little interest in continental politics,
and was resolved to have his own way in spite of the
Magnates, Parliament, or the People. His aim was
to free himself from the entanglement of foreign wars,
from popular pressure, and from Pitt. His first act
was to call to the Cabinet Lord Bute, the favourite
of his mother, whom he at once made his chief counsellor and agent. George's first speech to his Council
was drawn up by Bute, without concert with Pitt or
other ministers. As spoken, it talked of "a bloody
and expensive war, and of obtaining an honourable
and lasting peace." Sentiments in themselves sound,
and now shared by the better part of the nation; but
manifestly aimed at the policy of the great minister.
Pitt at once went to Bute and, after a long altercation,
had the printed report of the King's speech changed

to "an expensive, but just and necessary war"; and, after *honourable peace*, he got inserted the words "in. concert with our allies."

In a few months Lord Bute was made Secretary of State conjointly with Pitt, and virtually displacing him; Legge was dismissed from the Exchequer; and the whole Cabinet, except Lord Temple, were preparing to make an end both of war and of Pitt. France was now opening negotiations for peace. Whether these were sincere may be doubted, as the French minister, the Duc de Choiseul, was at the same time making secret overtures to Spain to join France, and Spain was pressing France to continue the war. Pitt was willing to consider the French terms of treaty, which were on the basis of *uti possidetis*, but with different dates for India, America, and Europe (1st September, 1st July, 1st May, 1761). Whilst willing to send an envoy, Pitt pressed on the attack upon Belle Isle, a rocky island lying off the coast of Brittany. Worthless as it was in itself, its possession would be a standing humiliation to France, and would serve to blockade the Breton coast and the mouth of the Loire. Thither Pitt sent a squadron and an army of 12,000 men. After an obstinate defence the garrison of 3500 men capitulated and surrendered the island. With this fresh conquest in his hands, Pitt offered peace on the terms of *uti possidetis*, either on the signature of the treaty or for the dates of 1st July, 1st September, and 1st November. Long pourparlers and reciprocal offers and concessions passed between Paris and London, in which it may be doubted if either side was quite sincere. When

Choiseul demanded the restitution of Cape Breton at the mouth of the St. Lawrence, and Pitt insisted on continuing to support Prussia in arms, it may be taken that the two diplomatists were playing a game of bluff.

At the end of July, Pitt's demands for a Treaty were :—

(1) The cession of all Canada, its dependencies, and all islands in the Gulf and river of St. Lawrence, with the exclusive right of fishing there. He rejected the French terms as to Louisiana.

(2) The cession by France of Senegal and Goree in Africa.

(3) Dunkirk to be reduced as stipulated at Utrecht in 1713.

(4) Equal partition of the four Neutral Islands in the West Indies.

(5) The island of Minorca to be restored to England.

(6) All French conquests in Germany, whether taken from Hesse, Brunswick, Hanover, or Prussia, *to be restored* and evacuated.

In return England would surrender the islands of Belle Isle, and Guadeloupe and Marie Galante in the West Indies.

These terms, as might be expected, were rejected by France.

Pitt held firm, resolved that "no Peace of Utrecht should stain the annals of England," continuing to use the imperious tone in which he had received all overtures. And he now became aware that an attempt was being made to drag Spain into the quarrel. Choiseul, indeed, committed the fatal blunder of insisting that Spain as well as France had grievances to be redressed. He had the impudence to send a dispatch formulating a series of demands on behalf of Spain. It was indeed a gross diplomatic offence for France, when treating for peace, to propose new hostile demands in the name of a power with whom England was ostensibly on friendly terms. Whether definitely so informed or not, Pitt divined the existence of concert between the powers. His indignation boiled over in language which he might have used to Newcastle or to Fox, but which was strange to the conventions of diplomatic intercourse. "His Majesty will not suffer the disputes with Spain to be blended in any manner whatever in the negotiation of peace between the two Crowns.—It will be considered an affront to His Majesty's dignity. *It is expected that France will not at any time presume a right of intermeddling in such disputes between Great Britain and Spain.*"

Pitt now saw clearly that neither France nor Spain desired peace on any terms which he would accept. And, in fact, on 15th August the "Family Compact" was signed. It was nothing less than an offensive and defensive alliance between the two Bourbon Monarchies, binding them to make no terms with their common enemies except by common consent. And, by a separate and secret treaty, Spain undertook, in exchange for the restoration of Minorca by France, to declare war on England on 1st May 1762, if France and England should be then engaged in hostilities. This was in fact the very alliance of the House of

Bourbon which had led to the War of the Spanish Succession. The treaty and its terms were kept secret; but Pitt soon understood its meaning; and, by the middle of September, he was warned by his agents of the preparations for war then being made in Spain.

He immediately broke off the negotiations with France, recalled his envoy from Paris, and dismissed the French envoy from London. Pitt now kept strictly in his own hands the negotiations which had been protracted for some four months. They are very intricate and continually varied, raising many important problems, amongst them the Newfoundland Fisheries question, which has embarrassed diplomacy for some two centuries and was settled only in our own day. But it is not necessary here to describe these elaborate negotiations, in which France was not well served, and England was represented by a man of imperious nature and insatiable patriotism. Choiseul was no doubt anxious to save his king and country in their desperate strait, but he was not willing to pay Pitt's price, which meant the sacrifice of all France had won in Germany as well as of all she had lost in the Far East and the Far West. With Pitt the *sine qua non* of peace involved the upholding of Frederick of Prussia. On that he wrote, "his Majesty's intentions will be found fixed and unalterable." With Choiseul, the *sine qua non* was the vindication of Maria Theresa, the maintenance of the House of Bourbon, and the means of restoring the French navy. Pitt was ready to settle all extra-European questions, provided they could be arranged so as to secure the triumphs of his country in war. He would not make a fresh Peace of Utrecht, nor would he abandon Frederick. And the suggestion of a conspiracy to found a new Bourbon preponderance in Europe roused him to fierce indignation.

Not content with breaking off negotiations with France, Pitt insisted on declaring war with Spain. Macaulay has pronounced this to be "a wise and resolute counsel"; and, from the point of view of increasing the ascendency of Britain it was not only this, but almost inevitable. Pitt urged that Spain was manifestly preparing for war, her treasure-ships and merchantmen could be seized on their way to Europe and would defray the cost of the war, and her American colonies could be seized without any new armaments. He conceived a grand scheme to despoil Spain of her colonies as he had despoiled France of hers. He arranged for a descent on Panama, and thence the conquest of Spanish America; from that he would seize Havannah, the Philippine Islands, and Manilla. On 18th September 1761 he represented to the Council his purpose of immediate war with Spain. "If any war could provide its own resources," he said, "it was war with Spain. Her supplies lay at a distance, and as we were masters of the sea, might easily be cut off." "Such a bold but necessary procedure would teach not only Spain but Europe the dangerous presumption of dictating to Great Britain." Louis le Grand in all his glory, befooled by all his flatterers, had hardly used bigger words. But, as Pitt himself said in later years, "the Council trembled." All members of the Cabinet, except Temple, raised objections to a new war.

The Cabinet delayed, and held three adjourned sittings. Pitt pressed his views with renewed energy.

"This was the time for humbling the whole House of Bourbon; if this opportunity were neglected, it might never be recovered; and, if he could not prevail in this instance, it was the last time he should sit in council. He thanked the ministers of the late King [not those brought in by George III.] for their support; he was himself called to the ministry by the voice of the people, to whom he considered himself accountable for his conduct; and he would no longer remain in a situation which made him responsible for measures which he was no longer allowed to guide."

This was in the vein of Scipio Africanus before the Senate, or of Oliver Cromwell dismissing the Long Parliament, rather than the tone of a constitutional minister in a Cabinet Council. On this occasion his colleagues do not seem to have "trembled," but they refused to follow him. And the President, the veteran Carteret-Granville, is said to have retorted, "that he was not sorry the gentleman would leave them, as in any other case they would have to leave him. When he talks of being responsible to the people, he talks the language of the House of Commons, and forgets that at this board he is only responsible to the King." We have no proof that either of these speeches was correctly reported. But in substance they represent the conflicting views of Pitt and his colleagues. On 5th October 1761 Pitt and Lord Temple resigned their places, after submitting their views in a written paper to the King.

This was a truly momentous event, affecting the history of Britain, of Europe, and even of the world. The passion and folly of the new King of Spain and the blind ambition of Spanish and French ministers made a Spanish war inevitable. Within a few months Spain herself declared war, in spite of the pacific tendencies of George III. and his new advisers. In that war not a few of the schemes planned by Pitt and the results he had foreseen actually took effect. The pride of France would not brook, in spite of all her disasters and her exhaustion, to surrender all her colonies as well as all she had fought for in Europe; to give up all her hopes of founding a great Eastern and a great Western Empire, and at the same time to suffer Prussia to rise to the position of a first-class power in Germany. That, however, was exactly what Pitt was resolved to effect. Nor can it be doubted that, if circumstances had favoured him, this result would have been effected far more completely than it was.

The position of Great Britain at the close of the year 1761 was one of absolute dominion of the seas to an extent hardly ever equalled before or since. Having 150 ships of the line, besides fleets of lesser vessels, manned by nearly 80,000 seamen, who were at that period without any rivals, England was perfectly secure at home, whilst she held the commerce of the seas and all transoceanic settlements within her grasp. No other nation possessed even the nucleus of marine power; and all were debarred from reaching such colonies as they still retained. Had George II. lived a few years longer, had Pitt maintained his health, his influence with the King, Parliament, and the Nation, it was quite probable that every possession of France, Spain, or Holland, outside of Europe, would have passed to the British Crown, and that these countries would have been forced to make peace on terms of extreme humiliation.

Britain alone was neither exhausted nor drained of money or of men. A war to conquer commerce and colonies, rather than settled territories, not only paid its own way, but was actually a new source of wealth and strength. The crowning victory of Quiberon Bay, where the fleet of France was annihilated, had cost us but forty lives. Had Pitt been suffered to seize the Spanish treasure ships, he would have paid the cost of the war with Spain twice over. British trade and prosperity had never risen so high as during the war. When the City of London carved on the monument of Pitt the memorable words that "commerce had been made to flourish by war," it was not at all an idle boast. It was recognised as a fact by another generation after Pitt's death. The supplies voted for 1761 were nearly £20,000,000—*i.e.* nearly twice as much as was voted in 1758, and £4,000,000 more than the votes for 1760. In Walpole's time they had been £8,000,000.[1] Everything points to the conclusion that if Pitt had retained his authority and his mental force for a short period more, he would have raised the ascendency of his country to a point of pre-dominance of which modern history has but rare examples.

Whether this result would have promoted the cause of civilisation, or even the ultimate good of our own country, is a very different thing. Any attempt to crush back the rival nations of Europe into a secondary

---

[1] Pitt's war policy had raised the National Debt from £70,000,000 to £150,000,000.

rank, to maintain a permanent and exclusive domination on the high seas, must at last evoke a combined
resistance, and in the end must exhaust an island of
moderate size. The morality of such a national policy
cannot now be defended or excused. All that can be
said is that the standards of the eighteenth century
were not those of the twentieth century, even after
all the debasement these standards have suffered of
late.   In that age of furious colonial rivalries, of
visions of transoceanic dominion, all nations possess-
ing seacoasts and maritime facilities and people, were
equally eager to found an empire. The advantages
of geography, our national faculties, free institutions,
and teeming population, enjoyed by Great Britain,
secured her in the hands of a great man a rapid
and splendid triumph. But neither the statesmen of
France or Spain, and assuredly no prince of any
Hohenzollern, Bourbon, or Hapsburg House, could
cast the first stone at Pitt.

He has been charged with being drunk with war,
delighting in war for itself ; but this is a gross
caricature of Pitt's ambition. Pitt himself saw no
fighting, and had no such thirst for battle as consumed
Alexander or Napoleon. The latter part of his life
was filled with strenuous opposition to war and to
exclusive domination. Pitt had no love of war. He
loved his country with passion ; and his ambition
was to make his country the first in the world, to
hand on to generations to come a mighty and stable
inheritance.   It was the ambition of Frederick, of
Marlborough, of Dupleix, of Lally, of Montcalm, of
Choiseul, of Alberoni, as it was of Pitt. But of them

all, Frederick and Pitt alone have founded vast empires which, after one hundred and forty years of growth, are still growing to-day.

In the *Annual Register* for 1761, Edmund Burke wrote: "Under him for the first time administration and popularity were seen united. . . . Alone this Island seemed to balance the rest of Europe. He revived the military genius of our people; he supported our allies; he extended our trade; he raised our reputation; he augmented our dominions."

Our own generation has so long forgotten the real conditions of 1761, and has so much overrated the blundering exploits of the puny imitators of Pitt, that it may be well to recall the famous peroration of Macaulay, for his words are as literally true as they are eloquent and just.

"The situation which Pitt occupied at the close of the reign of George the Second was the most enviable ever occupied by any public man in English history. He had conciliated the King; he domineered over the House of Commons; he was adored by the people; he was admired by all Europe. He was the first Englishman of his time; and he had made England the first country in the world. The Great Commoner, the name by which he was often designated, might look down with scorn on coronets and garters. The nation was drunk with joy and pride. . . . Whigs and Tories, Churchmen and Puritans, spoke with equal reverence of the Constitution, and with equal enthusiasm of the talents, virtues, and services of the Minister."

Walpole tells us that, on Pitt's fall, it was difficult

I

to say "which exulted most, France, Spain, or Bute."
"The nation was thunderstruck, alarmed, and indignant." When Pitt resigned the seals, the King received him graciously and offered him any rewards in the power of the Crown to grant. Surprised at such a reception, he burst into tears. "Pardon me, Sir," he said, "such goodness overpowers, it oppresses me." With his excitable temperament, with the extravagant reverence he felt for Majesty, the young George's manner had touched a genuine chord in Pitt's heart; but he made no demand. Bute pressed him to accept the governorship of Canada, with a salary of five thousand pounds, or the chancellorship of the Duchy, with its large salary. Pitt refused these or any other office. Nor would he accept a peerage. He agreed to accept the title of Baroness of Chatham for his wife and a pension of £3000 a year for his own and two lives.

At the time and since, much satire has been heaped on Pitt for his deigning to accept a title and a pension. It was thought that he who had talked so loud against the system of buying political support, and about his own dependence on the people, not on the Court, would have disdained such common rewards. As Burke says, "a torrent of low and illiberal abuse was poured out." His scandalous sister, Anne, maliciously reminded him that, when she herself had obtained a pension by truckling to Bute, he had replied that "he grieved to see the name of Pitt in the list of pensions." This was a nasty riposte, but the pensions given to Anne and to William Pitt had not been earned in exactly the same way.

The idea of William Pitt having ever been influenced by the pension was absurd, and his whole after life refuted it. And Burke is undoubtedly right in saying that "it is a shame that any defence should be necessary." Lord Holderness, a great peer and a nonentity, received on his retirement from the same office a pension of £4000. The grant of a pension for public services on retirement was in those days almost universal; and in our own days it is common enough. Pitt had devoted his whole life to the public service for twenty-four years, since he had been summarily dismissed from the army. He had no fortune, and he had rejected the possible means of making a fortune. He was married to a lady born and bred in a family of rank and wealth. The public idea of his Roman austerity and independence was honourable to him—but to such a man as Pitt wildly chimerical. Though in public life he was as haughty and as masterful as Coriolanus, he was by no means in private life a Cincinnatus who could plough his own humble furrow at home. He valued what Disraeli has praised in the nobles of our day, "the cultured magnificence of their stately lives." Everything about Pitt was grandiose—his mansion, his equipage, his footmen, his liveries, and his plate. In private as in public expenditure he was all through his life utterly reckless, and indifferent to cost. Lavish display was the almost universal habit of all public personages in the eighteenth century not only in England, but throughout Europe. Walpole, Chesterfield, Newcastle, Fox, Temple, Granville, all lived the lives of splendid magnates, as did the *grands seigneurs* and prelates of France, Spain, Italy, or Germany. Frederick, Turgot, Washington, Burke, were the few exceptions. They were rare instances of men in power who chose to live with great moderation. And it is clear that Pitt, popular tribune as he claimed to be, never aspired to be one of those noble examples of Spartan simplicity and plain living.

Much too has been said of the abject servility in the language Pitt used on the acceptance of his dignities. He threw himself " at the royal feet "—he was " penetrated with the bounteous favour of a most benign sovereign and master." He has not words to express his gratitude for the "unbounded grace of the most benign of sovereigns "—who had just kicked his great servant out of his sight. He even assures Lord Bute "of the value he puts on the favourable sentiments he had shown," in intriguing the dismissal. We do not use such language now. But it was the "common form" of that age. Pitt's bow was always the most profound and ceremonious at Court. The wits said "you could see his hook nose between his legs." If he entered the Royal closet he fell on his knees. The least peep into the closet, said Burke, intoxicates him. His letters of ordinary compliment were cast in that Ciceronian, or rather Grandisonian, solemnity which was the keynote of his written style. Nearly all the men of that age were grossly addicted either to pomp or to grandiloquence : some to both. But it must be allowed that Pitt very largely overdid the practice of his time.

Macaulay's famous rebuke is hardly too severe— " Pitt was an almost solitary instance of a man of real genius, and of a brave, lofty, and commanding spirit,

without simplicity of character." Pitt certainly was
not simple, but it would be absurd to say that one who
is not simple cannot be great or magnanimous. In
the age of Louis XIV., of Chesterfield, of Marlborough,
the golden age of the Dukes and Princes of Europe,
what was called "a fine manner" was not only
regarded as a merit in itself, but was a real source
of power to those who chose to use it. Some really
great men and some men of genius have deliberately
cultivated the theatric arts. Alexander, Napoleon.
Elizabeth, Richelieu, Byron, Chateaubriand, Victor
Hugo, were not exactly simple, nor always natural.
Pitt perhaps was never simple except with his children.
But it would be a mistake to judge him by this somewhat petty foible. It is a mark of meanness to make
too much fuss about mean things. Satirists who know
nothing of Pitt's great achievements, dish up for us
the scandalous epigrams of Walpole and Macaulay
about his crutch, his flannels, and his black velvet
suit. Pitt did not like to be caught in the grotesque
dishabille of an invalid. Even Julius Cæsar liked to
cover his bald head with a wreath.

Bute took care to have Pitt's honour and pension
announced in the Gazette along with his retirement.
Libels, insults, and merriment poured forth from his
enemies, but his friends and the City of London stood
by his side. The citizens pressed him to attend the
Guildhall banquet; and the restless and tactless
Temple persuaded him to go in a somewhat ostentatious way in the Earl's chariot. King George and his
young bride were received with chilling silence. The
fallen minister was hailed with roars of delight, which

were resumed in the Guildhall, with rounds of cheers led by Alderman Beckford, the Lord Mayor of 1762. The royal guests were ignored ; riots ensued in the streets ; gross caricatures were displayed ; and Bute was only saved from violence by being guarded by a gang of hired bruisers.

Pitt's conduct after his fall was restrained and magnanimous. As Burke said, " it set a seal on his character." And Macaulay declares that his genius and virtue never shone so brightly as during the session of 1762. He forbore to attack the colleagues who had ejected him. He even supported them. He avoided any claim to exclusive merit in all the successes past. · When the government was forced into war with Spain, he disclaimed any triumph. He urged unanimity. " The moment was come for every man to show himself for the whole. Be one people ! Forget everything but the public !—for the public I forget both my wrongs and my infirmities." He protested against abandoning the King of Prussia. " If our troops were recalled from Germany, he himself would be robbed of his honour, as the fear of it had already robbed him of his sleep. If we abandoned our allies, God would abandon us." "*America had been conquered in Germany.*" " Prince Ferdinand had been the saviour of Europe, and had shattered the whole military power of that military monarchy, France. If every other man in the House should be against the German war, he would stand single, and undergo the shame." Such was the passion that Pitt threw into the cause of aiding the newly formed kingdom of Prussia.

And now Pitt's anticipations were verified. Spain having got the treasure-ships safe into Cadiz changed her tone, haughtily refused to divulge the "Family Compact," recalled her ambassador and opened war. France and Spain in concert invaded Portugal, our ally. The last dispatch of the Spanish ambassador is described by Pitt's biographer as "his Catholic Majesty's declaration of war against the person of William Pitt." It is indeed a singular document. The war in which Spain and England were about to be plunged, it said, was to be charged "only to the pride and to the unmeasurable (*sic*) ambition" of the man—who had ceased to hold office for three months. His Spanish Majesty complained "of the insulting manner in which all the affairs of Spain had been treated during Mr. Pitt's administration." As will be seen, Pitt had been for three or four months utterly powerless in the Council and Parliament of George III., —who was himself bent on peace, who had dismissed Pitt rather than enter into war.

War with Spain was declared on 4th January 1762. Although the ministry had been forced into it against their wish, and maintained it with half a heart, the spirit that Pitt had infused into the army and the navy, and the designs he had prepared, brought it to so triumphant a success that we are told the glorious campaign of 1762 was only inferior to that of 1759. Martinique and the French islands of Grenada, St. Lucia, and St. Vincent in the West Indies were captured. After a severe resistance, Havannah, the key of Cuba, was taken; and in the East the settlement of Manila and the Philippines. Five thousand men

and a fleet were sent to defend Portugal. The caustic
wit of Walpole put the public effervescence in an
epigram. The eloquence of Pitt, he wrote, shines
months after it has set, like an annihilated star. "I
tell you it has conquered Martinico. There is more
martial spirit in the Gazette than in half Thucydides.
The Romans were three hundred years in conquering
the world. We subdue the globe in three campaigns
—and a globe as big again." Sir R. Lyttelton at
Rome wrote that these successes astonished all Europe.
The Pope told an English gentleman that so great was
the national glory, "that he esteemed it the highest
honour to be born an Englishman." His Holiness
apparently was out of temper with his Catholic
Majesty.

France and Spain were now both ready for peace—
almost as ready as were King George and Bute.
England had neither been intimidated nor injured by
the "Family Compact."[1] In truth, the three nations
as well as their governments and sovereigns desired
rest. And the King of Sardinia practically acted as
mediator in the complicated settlement. The terms
were these :—

(1) France surrendered to England the island of
Minorca ; in Africa, Senegal ; in America, the islands
of Cape Breton, St. John, and all Canada ; in the
West Indies, Grenada, Dominica, St. Vincent, and
Tobago. She *evacuated* the conquests made on Prussian

---

[1] "The nation which won in this war was that which had used its
sea-power in peace to increase its wealth, and in war to enlarge its
empire by the number of its seamen and the extent of its seaboard
and base" (Mahan, *Sea-Power*, p. 328).

territory, and *restored* those in Hanover, Hesse, and
Brunswick. She agreed to reduce the new defences
of Dunkirk.

(2) On her side, England restored to France the
island of Belle Isle ; in India, Pondicherry and recent
conquests, but without forts ; in Africa, Goree ; in the
West Indies, the islands of Martinique, Guadeloupe,
Marie Galante, and St. Lucia. The French right of
fishery in Newfoundland was confirmed as in the old
treaties ; and the small islands adjoining, of St. Pierre
and Miquelon, were ceded to their fishermen to cure
their fish. France and England mutually agreed to
withdraw their troops from Germany. Frederick
was left to fight it out with Russia and Austria.

(3) On her side, Spain restored to Portugal all that
she had recently taken. She ceded to England the
province of Florida ; and in exchange received the
restoration of Havannah and of the Philippines.
She ceded the right to cut timber in Honduras, and
withdrew the truly preposterous claim she had set up
to rights of fishery in Newfoundland—a claim which
Pitt, in his tragedy-king vein, said he would only
acknowledge when the King of Spain had stormed the
Tower of London.

This famous Treaty of Paris of 1763 was on the
whole a gain to all the countries involved, and in its
general lines secured a long period of peace. It was
somewhat less favourable to England than the terms
which Pitt had demanded, and certainly much less
than those he would have demanded after the conquests
of 1762. In three points, Pitt would have exacted
higher terms. He would have retained the West

Indian Islands; he would have rejected the Newfoundland fishery claims of France as well as of Spain; he would not have abandoned Prussia. As to Spain, which practically ceded little after a disastrous war, Pitt would have held on to Cuba and the Philippines, which Spain has only lost in our own day. And it is significant that the fishery problem was still in debate with France after one hundred and forty years. Lord Chesterfield, in many ways the keenest and coolest brain of the age, said at the time that the fishery dispute would go on just as it did before and had done since 1713.

At the bar of humanity and civilisation it must be judged that the Peace was salutary and just. But we can understand the feelings of Pitt and those whom he inspired, that much which had been won by lavish sacrifice of blood and treasure was being flung away in the inglorious haste of the King and his creatures to obtain a free hand at home, and to establish a personal government of the Crown. Had Pitt retained his mastery of the state in 1761 and 1762, it is probable that he would have swept into the Empire all the colonies of France and Spain both in the East and in the West; and would have established a maritime tyranny against which the whole of Europe would have risen in just indignation. The narrowness rather than the humanity of George III., and the weakness rather than the wisdom of his ministers, saved Europe from this misfortune and England from this career of arrogant aggrandisement.

When the Peace came to be considered in Parliament, great anxiety existed in the government; for in

the trading classes and in London its terms were
thought to be inadequate, and the opposition of Pitt,
whom Chesterfield called *ipse agmen*, might undo the
work of months of negotiation.   Fox had been promoted to lead the House of Commons, as the Hector
who alone could meet Achilles in the open.   Vast sums
were spent in buying the votes of members, and all who
opposed the Court and Ministers were dismissed from
office by a monstrous wholesale proscription ranging
from dukes to office-porters.   A venal or terrorised
majority was first secured.   The debate opened, and
Pitt was said to be confined to his room with a severe
attack of gout.   But now the House was alarmed by a
loud shouting without.   The doors opened, and at the
head of a concourse of his friends was seen Mr. Pitt,
borne in the arms of his servants, who set him down
within the bar, and with the help of his crutch and
some friendly hands he crawled to his seat.   He was
dressed in black velvet, his legs wrapped in flannel,
buskins of black cloth on his feet, and thick gloves on
his hands.   His face was emaciated, and he had the
air of intense suffering.   His voice was low, and from
time to time he obtained the rare privilege of resuming
his seat, whilst continuing to speak.   His speech held
the House for three hours and a half.   In effect, he
spoke thus :—

"He said that, though suffering excruciating torture, he
came at the hazard of his life to raise his voice against a treaty
which obscured all the glories of the war, surrendered the
dearest interests of the nation, and sacrificed the public faith
by an abandonment of our allies.   He began with the Fisheries
in Newfoundland and the St. Lawrence.   The concession to
France would enable her to recover her marine and to regain

her sea-power. He would, if he could, have insisted on the entire and exclusive fishery for our country. Havannah was an important conquest. He would have made it earlier had he been allowed to act. With Havannah ours, all the Spanish treasures in America lay at our mercy. The acquisition of Florida was no equivalent for the cession of Cuba. He would have kept Guadaloupe, had he been free. But now they cede not only Guadaloupe, but Martinique also, nay St. Lucia, the only valuable one of the neutral islands. Why did they conquer Martinique if they meant to restore it? They 'had lost sight of the great fundamental principle that France is chiefly, if not solely, to be dreaded by us in the light of a maritime and commercial power.' The Fisheries and the West India Islands will one day enable her to become formidable to us at sea. If Britain retained the exclusive trade with the West Indies, with Africa, with India, she would gain immensely in wealth and in command of the seas. This they were handing over to France. As to Germany, it was the employment of the French army there which had enabled us to make our conquests in America. The gallant King of Prussia was fighting in the same cause as ourselves, and is suffering for us. There were now new powers in Europe. Holland and Sweden had declined, and Russia 'had started up in its own orbit extrinsically of all other systems; but gravitating to each according to the mass of attracting interests it contains.' (Surely a marvellous bit of insight in 1762!) 'Another power, against all human expectation, was raised in Europe in the House of Brandenburgh.' (Surely, insight no less remarkable!) 'The balance of power in Europe has been entirely altered.' 'The German war prevented the French from succouring her colonies and islands in America, in Asia, and in Africa. Our successes were uniform because our measures were vigorous.' The French marine indeed was ruined—they had not ten ships of the line fit for service—but there was Spain who had joined France, and there were Swedes, Genoese, Dutch, from whom France might hire ships. As to the desertion of the King of Prussia, it 'was insidious, tricking, base, and treacherous.' The Treaty had in it the seeds of future war. It restored the enemy to his former greatness. The gains were no equivalent to the surrender."

Such was the tremendous *delenda est Carthago* of the British Cato : a policy, clear, practicable, almost achieved, and which Pitt might have accomplished had circumstances permitted—for a time at least.[1] It was an appeal to systematise the exclusive trade monopolies in favour in that age. The fisheries of North America, the sugar, cotton, and products of the West Indies, the rich and varied trade of India, the slave markets of Africa, were all at our mercy. France and Spain had settlements in all four of these lands ; but the absolute mistress of the seas could tear them away, and could hold them against the world. Once having all the important transmarine colonies in her hands, she must, and she could, establish with them a strict monopoly of trade. The scheme was grand, or rather grandiose, as was everything of Pitt's. It was in strict accord with the economics of that age. Nor was it contrary to the morality of the age. It was not until fourteen years later that Adam Smith dispelled this dismal illusion, when he wrote :—

". . . To found a great empire for the sole purpose of raising up a people of customers, may at first sight appear a project fit only for a nation of shopkeepers. It is, however, a project altogether unfit for a nation of shopkeepers ; but extremely fit for a nation whose government is influenced by shopkeepers. *Such statesmen, and such statesmen only, are capable of fancying that they will find some advantage in employing the blood and treasure of their fellow-citizens, to found and maintain such an empire.*"

Pitt, alas ! was such a statesman. His was a govern-

[1] Captain Mahan has clearly shown that France lost India and Canada because she could not act at a distance by sea. And Britain lost her American Colonies from the same failure in 1781.

ment deeply influenced by the shopkeepers of London and Bristol. Fallacies die hard! And even in our own day we have seen shopkeepers masquerading as statesmen, or statesmen cajoling the shopkeepers, who are willing to employ the blood and treasure of their fellow-citizens in founding an empire on the antiquated sophism of patriotic trade under the national flag.

Pitt's grand schemes were defeated by the thirst of power in the young King and the venal arts of Bute and Fox; and it is well for us that they were defeated, vile as were the means and contemptible as were his rivals. The agony and exhaustion of the great orator were such that he left the House at once without voting, and was welcomed outside with a roar of applause. Three hundred and nineteen members voted for the Peace. Sixty-five, on the other side, said Walpole, " were *not bribed*." " Now," said the Princess of Wales, " my son *is* King of England."

CHAPTER VIII

IN OPPOSITION

THE conduct of the "Great Commoner" after his dismissal was what we now call non-benevolent neutrality. He made no attempt to form a party, to overturn the ministry, or to return to power. He was independent, critical, at times their friend, their candid protector, but always with a grand air of superior wisdom. Nor can we deny that he showed a superior wisdom, and a nature above that of the feeble and selfish jobbers who had displaced him. Bute was so intensely unpopular that he was not safe in the streets, and had not a friend outside his own creatures. The English public stormed at everything Scotch, and insulted every Scot. On his side Pitt abstained from attacking Bute, and publicly proclaimed his esteem for North Britain. When his brother-in-law and old colleague, George Grenville, deserted him, and was promoted to lead the House of Commons, Pitt bantered him with his contempt rather than crushed him with his indignation. When Pitt was invited to join a new ministry again, he showed no desire to do so. And even when the King in his bewilderment was willing to treat with his rejected servant, Pitt refused to have anything to

do with government, unless he could form a ministry
on his own terms by his own choice.

All this time Pitt was wont to treat his opponents
with an air of amused contempt, and the House of
Commons as a body to be rebuked rather than convinced. He was now the object of virulent abuse and
savage lampoons, inspired and paid for by his rivals
and the Court. He made no reply in public or in
private. In the House, an Irish free-lance, Colonel
Barré, instigated, says Walpole, by Bute and Fox,
made a furious attack on Pitt, calling him "a profligate minister, who had thrust himself into power on
the shoulders of the mob." In the next debate, Barré
renewed his philippic, and was openly supported by
Fox. Pitt made no reply. "The indignation of the
House," says Walpole, "showed that such savage war
was detested." "Barré was abhorred as a barbarian
irregular, and Fox, who had lent such kind assistance
to a ruffian, drew the chief odium on himself." In the
debate on the Peace, Pitt studiously avoided replying
to Grenville. But when, on the Budget proposals,
Grenville, in his languid, querulous tone, asked the
opposition to tell him "*where* the money could be got,"
Pitt, mimicking his accent, repeated the words of a
popular song—*Gentle Shepherd, tell me where!* Grenville
was furious—but Pitt rose, bowed, and went out.
Grenville never lost the nickname of the "Gentle
Shepherd."

Bute soon proved himself to be incompetent, unscrupulous, and shameless. When he called in Fox,
with promise of a peerage, to pull the Peace through
Parliament, he sanctioned the most monstrous system

of corruption and of intimidation ever known even in that century of bribery and outrage. He made a Chancellor of the Exchequer of Sir Francis Dashwood, an ignorant débauché, who had once been a Jacobite. When this besotted junto proposed an excise on cider, with a right of search, to be paid by the grower, the public wrath was as great as when Walpole almost ruined himself by his Bill for an Excise. Pitt again thundered against Excise in his old strain. "Every man's house was his castle." "Excise was odious and grievous to the dealer, but intolerable to the private person, whose house was to be invaded by the gaugers." Pitt might thunder, but he was powerless. Parliament voted the tax by overwhelming majorities. And Johnson, as we know, in his Dictionary defined Excise as "a hateful tax levied upon commodities and adjudged not by the common judges of property, but wretches hired by those to whom excise was paid." Pitt was not the only man in the eighteenth century who used violent phrases.

Violent language was now the order of the day, and no man used language so violent and coarse as the profligate and scurrilous wit, John Wilkes, member for Aylesbury, Colonel of the Bucks Militia, whose escapades were destined to throw into confusion, for many long years, governments, parties, and the Court. Wilkes, a man ruined and infamous, but still popular in many brilliant circles, had founded the *North Briton*, wherein he criticised by name public persons with an audacity and insolence that were unknown even in that age. In Number 45, after exhausting the language of insult to the Scots and the Scottish minister, Wilkes attacked the King's speech, and lamented that the Sovereign's name should give sanction "to the most odious measures," "most unjustifiable doctrines," and "infamous fallacy," and so forth, in a strain in which ministers were often assailed in those days—and indeed in our own. Walpole said "nothing could be more just than the satire." The government committed the folly of seizing Wilkes, searching his house and papers, under a *general* (*i.e.* an open) warrant without name, and committed him to the Tower. The defeat of "general warrants" in the courts of law, the triumph of Wilkes, and the blundering illegalities committed by the ministers at the King's desire, form a memorable chapter in the history of Parliament and the doctrine of the Constitution, and need not be here rehearsed.

When the matter came before Parliament, Pitt made an admirable speech, defending the great constitutional principles with weighty good sense, and lucidly expounding the legal grounds on which they rest. Racked as he was with gout, he said :—

" The surrender of the privileges of a member was dangerous to the freedom of Parliament, and an infringement on the rights of the people. It put every member who did not vote with the minister under a perpetual terror of imprisonment. If a member committed a crime, Parliament would not shield him ; but Parliament had no right to vote away its privileges. The paper no doubt was a libel—he entirely agreed. He condemned the whole series of the " *North Britons* "; he called them illiberal, unmanly, and detestable. He abhorred all reflections of a nation. The King's subjects were one people. Whoever divided them was guilty of sedition. The author, it was true, was the blasphemer of his God, and the libeller of his King. The dignity and the honour of Parliament had

been called upon to support and protect the purity of his
Majesty's character ; and this they had done, by a strong and
decisive condemnation of the libel.   But having done this, it
was neither consistent with the honour and safety of Parliament, nor with the rights and interests of the people, to
go one step farther.   The rest belonged to the Courts
below."

Wilkes escaped to France, and in the next year he
was expelled from the House by what was afterwards
admitted to be an act *ultra vires*.   In the debate on the
legality of "general warrants," Pitt again spoke with
excellent sense and justice.   He challenged ministers
to defend the legality of such warrants.   To argue
that they had been issued by other governments was
no justification.   It was true that two such warrants
had been issued by himself.   But they were not
against libels.   Both were for the seizure of foreigners
about to leave the country.   Both were issued in a
time of war to apprehend enemies.   He had been
advised by the Attorney-General that the warrant was
illegal, and that he must take the consequences.   He
deliberately faced the risk, and, for the public safety,
he seized a suspicious foreigner who was in hiding.   In
the present case, there was no urgency or necessity.
The safety of the state was in no danger.   Parliament
had voted away its own privilege and laid the personal
freedom of every representative of the people at the
mercy of the Attorney-General.   The wanton exercise
of an illegal power admits of no justification or even
palliation.   In the present case it is personal resentment against a particular person.   If the House supported these general warrants, they would be the
disgrace of the present age and the reproach of

posterity. All this is now the unquestioned law of the Constitution.

In April 1763 Lord Bute astonished the world by sudden resignation of office. He had obtained everything he could hope to gain, and he shrank from the difficulties and the hatred with which he was surrounded. He no doubt fully counted on retaining power as royal Favourite, even if he publicly withdrew from office. He was succeeded by George Grenville, who, with sterling qualities of honesty, courage, and industry, had a singular gift of annoying the King and of blundering into dangerous crises. The ministry of Grenville, however, was as unstable and as unpopular as that of Bute, whilst it showed no willingness to submit to the voice that whispered behind the throne. Before five months had passed, the Favourite sought an interview with Pitt himself and suggested his laying his views before the King. Next day Pitt was summoned to the King's closet. The interview was outrageously irregular and indecent. At the instigation of the late Prime Minister, who had resigned office five months previously, *and unbeknown to the actual ministers for the time being*, King George held a long private interview with the former Prime Minister, whom he himself had dismissed less than two years before. And this took place at Buckingham House, and not at Versailles or Potsdam.

The King told Pitt that he thought his present ministers could not stand ; and he practically invited Pitt to suggest what ministry he would himself propose in their place. Pitt discussed the question in great detail, and evidently proposed a coalition with

Newcastle, Devonshire, Rockingham, Temple, and Hardwicke. In the first interview, the King seemed inclined to accept the combination. But reflection soon opened his eyes, and probably those of the Favourite, that what Pitt intended was a strong government of which he should be the master spirit. The negotiation was at once broken off. The King was resolved to be master: and Pitt was resolved not to be a tool. Throughout the negotiation Pitt had treated the King with grand deference; but frankly told him with whom he would serve, and with whom he would not serve. The King on his part was obstinate and prejudiced for and against persons, and wanted to form Pitt's ministry himself. On the rupture, he went about in his garrulous, mischief-making, self-sufficient way, throwing the failure on Pitt, and publicly naming the men in whom Pitt had expressed want of confidence. The shrewd Chester-field as usual summed up the whole situation in a phrase—"the one asked too much, and the other would not yield enough." Neither Pitt, nor George, was much given to yield—the one because he was too great, the other because he was too little, to take counsel of any one but himself.

Before we pass to the disasters and criminal blunders of the Grenville ministry, "the worst administration since the Revolution," as Macaulay says, and to the rickety ministry of the respectable Rockingham, who succeeded Grenville, it will be well to collect all the abortive attempts made to bring Pitt into office until he formed his second administration. The "cousin-hood" had long been broken up, and Lord Temple alone remained at Pitt's side. They also had begun to differ on many things, as about Wilkes. Without family influence, without a party, without regular followers in either house; a Whig by principle, but not a sworn partisan of that faction; a believer in personal government and a sentimental royalist, but yet not a Tory; a passionate stickler for the Constitution as settled in 1689 and for the sacred right of popular representation—Pitt, by the ascendency of his genius and character, seemed to make every government from which he was excluded a temporary expedient; and yet he had neither the desire nor the means to form a government of his own.

The King soon began to hate George Grenville as minister even more than Pitt; but after the failure of the negotiation with Pitt, he was forced to take Grenville back, with the Duke of Bedford as a sort of buffer. George then called in his uncle, the Duke of Cumberland, to his aid. The Duke made fresh overtures to Pitt, actually going down to Hayes to see the invalid in his sick-room. Pitt was prepared to form a ministry, "*if he could carry the constitution with him.*" By this he seems to have meant that the illegal doings and the proscriptions of Bute and Grenville should be reversed, the obnoxious taxes repealed, and no influence behind the throne suffered to interfere. Temple and Pitt were told that the King would insist on certain nominations to office; and thereupon, though Pitt seemed willing to yield, Temple peremptorily refused, and persuaded Pitt to do the same. The great rupture between Pitt and Temple had not yet come. Their close alliance in family and in politics had lasted for twenty years, and Temple was now the last remaining colleague that Pitt retained. Pitt, we are told, in his grand way, repeated the verses Anna uttered to Dido when she discovered the rash act :

> "Exstinxti me teque, soror, populumque patresque
> Sidonios, urbemque tuam."

It has been the fashion to condemn Pitt for refusing office on this occasion, and to ascribe it to his weakness in yielding his better judgment "to his evil genius, Temple." This is not quite so clear. The motives that swayed the harassed mind of the tortured proud man in the retirement of his chamber are even now far from plain. But if Pitt had reason to believe that the King and Bute, with their confederates, were still strong enough to tie his hands, he may have been right in refusing to help.

The King found Grenville intolerable, and struggled to discover a substitute to replace him. The great Whig nobles were hardly more tolerable, and one after another they caused a ministerial crisis by their unpopularity or by their exacting terms. No minister would satisfy King George, except one who would do the King's work by corruption or by illegalities. At each crisis he was forced to call back the capable and resolute man whom he personally hated. "I would sooner meet Mr. Grenville at the point of my sword than let him into my Cabinet," said George in his despair. The Duke of Bedford read the King a written lecture on his conduct so severe that George said if he had not broken out into a sweat he would have been suffocated with indignation. Again he got his uncle Cumberland to confer with Pitt. And again, we are told, Pitt refused at the instigation of "his evil genius," Temple. At last, after endless negotiations, offers, and refusals, the Marquis of Rockingham, in July 1765, formed an administration.

Lord Rockingham was a young, inexperienced, honest nonentity, of great position and blameless character, who had nothing to recommend him but rank, his good intentions, and the genius of Edmund Burke, his private secretary and real leader. The ministry he got together with prolonged effort was mainly drawn from the Whig magnates, including the veteran jobber Newcastle, one or two honourable and competent men, Townshend, an erratic meteor, and some of the old Court gang. Rockingham made every effort to persuade Pitt to join him; he had visited him in his sickroom at Hayes; he asked his advice before he made a plan; he solicited his help on three separate occasions; he invited Pitt's friends to take office. He seemed to offer Pitt not only office but the leadership of the whole party and government.

All this Pitt declined. Lord Hardwicke said, Pitt would "neither lead nor be driven." Burke put down the failure "to the intractable temper of your friend Pitt," who was "lying on his back at Hayes talking fustian." Lord Chesterfield, as usual, exactly spoke the right word when he said the ministry was an arch in which the keystone was left out, and of course the keystone was Pitt. Both in his own day and in ours Pitt has been loudly condemned for not joining Lord Rockingham in the feeble and shortlived ministry of 1765. Mr. Lecky tells us that this refusal, "if not the worst, was certainly the most disastrous incident of

Pitt's career." It is possible that the combination of Pitt, Burke, Conway, and the blameless Rockingham, might have made an efficient government in time, if Pitt had been allowed to lead. But Burke in 1765 had not spoken in Parliament; Rockingham never became able to speak in it at all; the old Newcastle, whom Pitt now utterly despised, was enrolled as a member of the new ministry; and Bute, as Pitt feared, was still behind the throne. Lastly, Pitt himself was "lying on his back at Hayes," tortured with his fell disease and constantly a prey to nervous irritation. We do not know enough to condemn him for refusing to join a ministry in which were to be retained some of the worst elements that he most abhorred, and wherein he had good reason to fear that the creatures of the King would continue to hold a secret and malign influence. But even if we knew, more exactly than we do, all that acted on his mind, it would not be just to treat it as a crime, if a man, in the throes of disease and confined to a sick-room in his country house, shrank from undertaking a public task of tremendous difficulty in company with men, some of whom he regarded as frankly mischievous and all of whom he regarded as utterly his inferiors. The early years of George III.'s reign were marked by a miserable succession of feeble and incoherent ministries. But the inner cause of all this confusion and failure was the perverse self-will and criminal ambition of George himself.

It is possible that a powerful and stable government might have been ultimately formed by a loyal combination of Pitt, Rockingham, Shelburne, Grafton,

Conway, and Burke—always assuming the quiescence of George III. and of gout. But this is all the "great-might-have-been." In 1765 neither Pitt nor any one else could have known the powers of Edmund Burke, as we know them now. And they were at best those of a philosopher rather than of a statesman. But cabinet-making one hundred and forty years after the date is an even more futile amusement than cabinet-making by contemporaries in a crisis. The photographic diaries of Walpole record at least six different occasions on which more or less formal negotiations were opened with Pitt, between 1762 and 1766, to induce him to form or to join a ministry. They prove at any rate that he was not eager to take office. We are in no position to determine that he failed in duty to his country by declining all these overtures. The better solution would seem to be that disease, with all its mental and moral reaction, had much to do with his conduct. And George III. was an obstacle even worse than the gout. Pitt perhaps wrote the truth when he said to Lord Shelburne (February 1766) that he would never owe his return to power "to any Court cabal or ministerial connection." All the dissolving ministries between 1761 and 1766 were patched up by one or other of these methods, and some of them by both.

At last, in July 1766, Pitt was almost forced by the state of the political imbroglio to form a second administration. But before treating of it, it will be well to go back to the brief ministries of Grenville and Rockingham to show the difficulties to which Pitt succeeded. In March 1764 Grenville carried a resolution to charge certain Stamp duties on the American colonies. It was the beginning of a struggle which was destined to dominate British policy for a generation, and indeed to affect for centuries the history of mankind. The Stamp Act of 1765 was calculated to raise £100,000, and it was proposed to expend it in contributing to the cost of the army needful to be kept in America. This, under the vastly enlarged area of the colonies, was taken to mean 20,000 men. The opposition on the other side of the Atlantic was at first not great. But in Parliament Conway and Barré raised objections. Pitt was absent from Parliament almost entirely during the year. He was laid up with recurrent attacks of gout from the time of his powerful speech in condemnation of General Warrants. In his own day and since some doubt has been expressed as to the degree to which at this period Pitt was incapacitated by his malady. A few facts about it may be here collected.

In January 1764 Charles, the heir of the Duke of Brunswick, desiring to pay a compliment and to visit the statesman, took the unusual course of going down to see him in the country, as he learned that there was no prospect of Pitt being able to be carried to town. In February 1765, Pitt writes to the secretary of the Duke that his gout had kept him in bed and prevented him from holding a pen. In November 1765 he goes again to Bath, and tells his wife that "the foot is much swelled, the hand less weak." "He can now hold a pen." "He can stand with the help of crutches." "He can hold a fork at dinner and can write legibly." In December, he can "crawl to the pump." In January 1766, if he can crawl or be carried to town, he will "deliver his mind and heart on the state of America." In the midst of the debate on the Stamp Act, he tells his wife that he is better except in one leg. He hopes "to be able to remain through the debate." In May 1766, he has to go to Bath again; and tells his wife "he had borne the journey well."

He was in the west country when, 7th July 1766, he received the King's command to travel up to Court to consult him as to a new ministry, as soon as he was strong enough. It was not till 12th July that he arrived in London, and tells his wife—"I got safe to town, not over well, having found the fatigue of the first day too much for me." On 17th July he tells his wife that he has some fever hanging on him, and a long and painful interview with his brother-in-law, Temple, had raised his pulse. On 19th July he trusts to be able next week to attend the King without risk. At last, 22nd July 1766, the King writes: "Mr. Pitt, I am glad you find yourself so much recovered as to be able to come to me to-morrow." Such was the physical state of the man whom George III. now summoned to direct his disordered affairs in his vast dominions. It was hoped that he would be strong enough to bear a journey of a mile or two to meet his sovereign. The life of Pitt cannot be understood at all unless we fully comprehend the constant prostration of body and mind which afflicted him throughout his career, and amply explains much in his conduct. Hardly any famous man of action in history has been so heavily and so continuously disabled by physical and mental disorder.

A man so delicate and irritable would naturally often
change his residence; and accordingly we find Pitt in
many different houses, and at no period of his life
more than at this time.   During his term of office
of Paymaster, 1746-1755, he lived much at the Pay
Office at Whitehall, and was there the first year of his
marriage.   He also had a house at Enfield in Middlesex, making frequent visits to Lord Temple at Stowe,
and to the Grenvilles at Wotton.   For the first six
months of 1754, the year of his marriage, he was at
Bath, taking the waters and very lame.

He told Grenville as early as 1749, that he had
"almost experience enough of the Bath waters to be a
physician with regard to them."   He passed much of
his life at various medicinal springs, and was at Bath
again in 1755.   In the spring of 1756 he is established at Hayes, a property which he bought soon
after his marriage.

Hayes Place in Kent stands on a salubrious and
well-wooded hill, about twelve miles from London,
and a few miles south of Bromley.   He built there
a comfortable country house of no great pretensions,
then standing close to a quiet village, having orna-
mental grounds, plantations, and pleasant views.   Pitt
gradually enlarged the place and carried on his
favourite amusement of landscape gardening, planting
shrubs and trees with the same passionate energy that
he threw into everything he touched.   He loved the
spot, and his letters show the affection for it that he
retained through life.   In 1766, being then settled at
Burton Pynsent, he sold Hayes Place to Thomas
Walpole, nephew of the statesman, who at once made

alterations in the house, which he greatly enjoyed. But within a year Lady Chatham and Lord Camden induced Mr. Walpole to sell back the place, which was thought to be indispensable for restoring Pitt's ruined health and disordered mind.

During his own ministry Pitt had lived in St. James's Square (No. 10), the house occupied for a season by Mr. Gladstone in 1890. When he resigned office in 1761, he resided at Hayes; but in 1766 and 1767 he took Northend House at Hampstead, the air of which, he thought, would suit his complaint. In 1765 Sir William Pynsent, a baronet of Somersetshire, said to be nearly ninety years old, and known to be eccentric and an ardent opponent of the government, devised to him the fine estate of Burton Pynsent, which was said to be of the value of £3000 a year, together with £30,000 in money, according to Walpole. Sir William Pynsent was personally unknown to Pitt, and the gift was entirely due to the donor's admiration of the statesman's services to his country. During his second ministry Pitt occupied for a time the mansion of the Duke of Grafton in Bond Street. But he soon retreated to the country, and after his resignation he continued to reside for the most part at his beloved Hayes Place. It was thither that he was carried after his seizure to his death-bed.

It may be taken as almost certain that, if Pitt had been in his place and in full possession of his powers, the disastrous policy of taxing the American colonies could not have been carried. But during the whole of the debates on Grenville's Stamp Act of 1765, Pitt was away at Bath, and disabled by gout. When

Lord Rockingham succeeded Grenville, one of his first
and most beneficial measures was the Repeal of the
Stamp Act, in 1766, and this was very largely due to
the influence and eloquence of Pitt. Up to the beginning of the year 1766 Pitt remained in retirement
at Bath. From there he wrote to Lord Shelburne
protesting against "the making good by force there,
preposterous and infatuated errors in policy here."
In January 1766 he returned to the House of
Commons after a long absence, with powers materially
restored. The King's Speech turned on the disturbed
state of the American colonies, where riots and
violent opposition made the Stamp Act wholly un-
workable. In fact, the American revolution was on
the point of breaking out eight years earlier than it
did. In the debates which brought about the Repeal
of the Stamp Act, Pitt had a leading part. As these
speeches are amongst the most authentic reports we
possess, and as they contain many of his noblest
utterances, it may be well to quote them at large :—

"Sir, I came to town but to-day. I was a stranger to the
tenor of his Majesty's speech and the proposed address, till I
heard them read in this House. Unconnected and uncon-
sulted, I have not the means of information ; I am fearful of
offending through mistake, and therefore beg to be indulged
with a second reading of the proposed address." The address
being read, Mr. Pitt went on :—"He commended the King's
speech, approved of the address in answer, as it decided
nothing, every gentleman being left at perfect liberty to take
such a part concerning America as he might afterwards see
fit. One word only he could not approve of ; 'an *early*' is a
word that does not belong to the notice the ministry have
given to Parliament of the troubles in America. In a matter
of such importance, the communication ought to have been

immediate : I speak not with respect to parties. I stand up in this place single and unconnected. As to the late ministry (turning himself to Mr. Grenville, who sat within one of him), every capital measure they took was—entirely wrong !

"As to the present gentlemen, those, at least, whom I have in my eye—(looking at the bench on which Mr. Conway sat with the Lords of the Treasury)—I have no objection ; I have never been made a sacrifice by any of them. Their characters are fair ; and I am always glad when men of fair character engage in his Majesty's service. Some of them have done me the honour to ask my poor opinion before they would engage. These will do me the justice to own, I advised them to engage, but notwithstanding—for I love to be explicit—I cannot give them my confidence ; pardon me, gentlemen (bowing to the Ministry), confidence is a plant of slow growth in an aged bosom, youth is the season of credulity ; by comparing events with each other, reasoning from effects to causes, methinks I plainly discover the traces of an *overruling influence.*

"There is a clause in the Act of Settlement obliging every Minister to sign his name to the advice which he gives his Sovereign. Would it were observed ! I have had the honour to serve the Crown, and if I could have submitted to *influence* I might still have continued to serve ; but I would not be responsible for others. I have no *local* attachments. It is indifferent to me whether a man was rocked in his cradle on this or that side of the Tweed. I sought for merit wherever it was to be found. It is my boast, that I was the first minister who looked for it, and found it in the mountains of the North. I called it forth, and drew into your service a hardy and intrepid race of men ; men who, when by your jealousy they became a prey to the artifices of your enemies, had gone nigh to overturn the State in the war of 1745. These men, in the last war, were brought to combat on your side ; they served with fidelity, as they fought with valour, and conquered for you in every part of the world ; detested be the national reflections against them ! they are unjust, groundless, illiberal, unmanly. When I ceased to serve his Majesty as a Minister, it was not the *country* but the *man* by which I was moved. The *man* of that country [Bute] wanted wisdom, and held principles incompatible with freedom.

"It is a long time, Mr. Speaker, since I have attended in Parliament. When the resolution was taken in this House to tax America, I was ill in bed. If I could have endured to have been carried in my bed, so great was the agitation of my mind for the consequences, I would have solicited some kind hand to have laid me down on this floor, to have borne my testimony against it ! It is now an Act that has passed. I would speak with decency of every Act of this House, but I must beg the indulgence of the House to speak of it with freedom.

"I hope the day may soon be appointed to consider the state of the nation with respect to America—I hope gentlemen will come to this debate with all the temper and impartiality that his Majesty recommends, and the importance of the subject requires. *A subject of greater importance than ever engaged the attention of this House!* that subject only excepted, when, near a century ago, it was the question whether you yourselves were to be bond or free. In the mean time, as I cannot depend upon health for any future day, such is the nature of my infirmities, I will beg to say a few words at present, leaving the justice, the equity, the policy, the expediency of the Act to another time. I will only speak to one point, a point which seems not to have been generally understood—I mean *as to the right to tax.* Some gentlemen seem to have considered it as a point of honour. If gentlemen consider it in that light, they leave all measures of right and wrong to follow a delusion that may lead to destruction. It is my opinion, that *this Kingdom has no right to lay a tax upon the colonies.* At the same time I assert the authority of this kingdom over the colonies to be sovereign and supreme in every circumstance of government and legislation whatsoever. The colonists are the subjects of this kingdom, equally entitled with yourselves to all the natural rights of mankind and the peculiar privileges of Englishmen : equally bound by its laws, and equally participating in the constitution of this free country. The Americans are the sons, not the bastards, of England. *Taxation is no part of the governing or legislative power. The taxes are the voluntary gift and grant of the Commons alone.* In legislation the three estates of the realm are alike concerned, but the concurrence of the Peers and the Crown to a tax is only necessary to clothe it with the *form* of a law. The *gift* and *grant* is of

L

the Commons *alone*. In ancient days, the Crown, the Barons, and the Clergy possessed the lands. In those days, the Barons and the Clergy gave and granted to the Crown. They gave and granted what was their own. At present, since the discovery of America, and other circumstances permitting, the Commons are become the proprietors of the land. The Church (God bless it!) has but a pittance. The property of the Lords, compared with that of the Commons, is as a drop of water in the ocean : and this House represents those Commons, the proprietors of the lands, and those proprietors virtually represent the rest of the inhabitants. When, therefore, in this House, we give and grant, we give and grant what is our own. But in an American tax, what do we do? We, your Majesty's Commons for Great Britain, give and grant to your Majesty—what? Our own property?—No! We give and grant to your Majesty, the property of your Majesty's Commons of America. It is an absurdity in terms.

" *The distinction between legislation and taxation is essentially necessary to liberty*. The Crown, the Peers, are equally legislative powers with the Commons. If taxation be a part of simple legislation, the Crown and the Peers *would have rights in taxation as well as yourselves* ; rights which they claim, which they will exercise, whenever the principle can be supported by *power*.

"There is an idea in some, that the colonies are virtually represented in this House. I would fain know by whom an American is represented here. Is he represented by any knight of the shire, in any county of this kingdom? Would to God that respectable representation were augmented to a greater number! Or will you tell him that he is represented by any representative of a borough?—a borough which perhaps its own representatives never saw. This is what is called *the rotten part of the constitution*. *It cannot continue a century*. *If it does not drop, it must be amputated*. The idea of a virtual representation of America in this House is the most contemptible that ever entered into the head of man : it does not deserve a serious refutation.

"The Commoners of America, represented in their several assemblies, have ever been in possession of the exercise of this their constitutional right, of giving and granting their own money.   They would have been slaves if they had not enjoyed it.   At the same time this Kingdom, as the supreme governing and legislative power, has always bound the colonies by her laws, by her regulations and restrictions in trade, in navigation, in manufactures—in everything except that of taking their money out of their pockets without their consent.

"Here I would draw the line,

'*Quam ultra citraque nequit consistere rectum.*'"

Pitt was answered by Grenville.   In his reply, he said:—

"Gentlemen have been charged with giving birth to sedition in America.   Several have spoken their sentiments with freedom against this unhappy Act, and that freedom has become their crime.   Sorry I am to hear the liberty of speech in this House imputed as a crime.   But the imputation shall not discourage me.   It is a liberty I mean to exercise.   No gentleman ought to be afraid to exercise it.   It is a liberty by which the gentleman who calumniates it might have profited.   He ought to have profited.   He ought to have desisted from his project.   The gentleman tells us America is obstinate; America is almost in open rebellion.   *I rejoice that America has resisted.   Three millions of people so dead to all the feelings of liberty, as voluntarily to let themselves be made slaves, would have been fit instruments to make slaves of all the rest.*   I come not here armed at all points with law cases and Acts of Parliament, with the statute-book doubled down in dogs'-ears, to defend the cause of liberty: if I had, I myself would have cited the two cases of Chester and Durham.   I would have cited them to show that, even under arbitrary reigns, Parliaments were ashamed of taxing a people without their consent, and allowed them representatives.   Why did the gentleman confine himself to Chester and Durham?   he might have taken a higher example in Wales—Wales, that never was taxed by Parliament until it was incorporated.   I would not debate a particular point of law with the gentleman: I know his abilities.   I have been obliged to his diligent researches.   But, for the defence of liberty, upon a general principle, upon a constitutional principle, it is a ground on which I stand firm;

on which I dare meet any man. The gentleman tells us of
many who are taxed and are not represented—the India Company, merchants, stockholders, manufacturers. Surely many
of these are represented in other capacities, as owners of land,
or as freemen of boroughs. *It is a misfortune that more are not
actually represented.* But they are all inhabitants of this
kingdom, and, as such, are they not virtually represented?
Many have it in their option to be actually represented. They
have connections with those that elect, and they have influence
over them. The gentleman mentioned the stockholders : I
hope he does not reckon the debts of the nation as a part of
the national estate. Since the accession of King William,
many ministers, some of great, others of moderate abilities,
have taken the lead of government.

" None of these thought, or even dreamed, of robbing the
colonies of their constitutional rights. That was reserved to
mark the era of the late administration ; not that there were
wanting some, when I had the honour to serve his Majesty,
to propose to me to burn my fingers with an American Stamp
Act. With the enemy at their back, with our bayonets at
their breasts in the day of their distress, perhaps the Americans
would have submitted to the imposition ; but it would have
been taking an ungenerous and unjust advantage. The gentleman boasts of his bounties to America ! Are not those bounties
intended finally for the benefit of this kingdom? If they are
not, he has misapplied the national treasures. I am no courtier
of America—I stand up for this kingdom. I maintain that
the Parliament has a right to bind, to restrain America. Our
legislative power over the colonies is sovereign and supreme.
When it ceases to be sovereign and supreme, I would advise
every gentleman to sell his land, if he can, and embark for
that country. When two countries are connected like England
and her colonies, without being incorporated, the one must
necessarily govern ; the greater must rule the less ; but so rule
it, as *not to contradict the fundamental principles that are
common to both.*

" If the gentleman does not understand the difference
between internal and external taxes, I cannot help it ; but
there is a plain distinction between taxes levied for the purposes of raising a revenue, and duties imposed for the regulation

of trade, for the accommodation of the subject; although in the consequences some revenue might incidentally arise from the latter.

"The gentleman asks, When were the colonies emancipated? I desire to know when they were made slaves? But I dwell not upon words. When I had the honour of serving his Majesty, I availed myself of the means of information which I derived from my office: I speak, therefore, from knowledge. My materials were good; I was at pains to collect, to digest, to consider them; and I will be bold to affirm that the profits of Great Britain from the trade of the colonies, through all its branches, are two millions a year. This is the fund that carried you triumphantly through the last war. The estates that were rented at two thousand pounds a year, threescore years ago, are at three thousand pounds at present. Those estates sold then for from fifteen to eighteen years' purchase; the same may now be sold for thirty. You owe this to America. This is the price America pays for her protection. *And shall a miserable financier come with a boast, that he can fetch a peppercorn into the Exchequer, by the loss of millions to the nation!* I dare not say how much higher these profits may be augmented. Omitting the immense increase of people by natural population, in the northern colonies, and the emigration from every part of Europe, I am convinced that the whole commercial system of America may be altered to advantage. You have prohibited where you ought to have encouraged; and you have encouraged where you ought to have prohibited. *Improper restraints have been laid on the continent in favour of these islands.* You have but two nations to trade with in America. Would you had twenty! Let Acts of Parliament in consequence of treaties remain, but let not an English minister become a custom-house officer for Spain, or for any foreign power. Much is wrong— much may be amended for the general good of the whole.

"Does the gentleman complain that he has been misrepresented in the public prints? It is a common misfortune. In the Spanish affair of last war, I was abused in all the newspapers for having advised his Majesty to violate the Law of Nations with regard to Spain. The abuse was industriously circulated even in handbills. If your administration did not propagate the abuse, the administration never contradicted it.

I will not say what advice I did give to the King. My advice is in writing signed by myself, in the possession of the Crown. But I will say what advice I did not give to the king. *I did not advise him to violate any of the Laws of Nations.*

"The gentleman must not wonder that he was not contradicted when, as the minister, he asserted the right of Parliament to tax America. I know not how it is, but there is a modesty in this House which does not choose to contradict a minister. Even that chair, Mr. Speaker, *sometimes looks towards St. James's.* I wish gentlemen would get the better of this modesty. If they do not, perhaps the collective body may begin to abate of its respect for the representative.

"A great deal has been said without doors of the power, of the strength, of America. It is a topic that ought to be cautiously meddled with. In a good cause, on a sound bottom, the force of this country can crush America to atoms. I know the valour of your troops; I know the skill of your officers. There is not a company of foot that has served in America, out of which you may not pick a man of sufficient knowledge and experience to make a governor of a colony there. But on this ground—on the Stamp Act—when so many here will think it is a crying injustice, I am one who will lift up my hands against it.

"*In such a cause even your success would be hazardous. America, if she fell, would fall like the strong man Samson.* She would embrace the pillars of the State, and *pull down the constitution along with her.* Is this your boasted Peace? To sheathe the sword, not in its scabbard, but in the bowels of your countrymen? Will you quarrel *with yourselves,* now that the whole House of Bourbon is united against you? While France disturbs your fisheries in Newfoundland, embarrasses your slave-trade to Africa, and withholds from your subjects in Canada their property stipulated by treaty; while the stipulated ransom for the Manilas is refused by Spain, and its gallant conqueror basely traduced into a mean plunderer—a gentleman whose noble and generous spirit would do honour to the proudest grandee of the country. The Americans have not acted in all things with prudence and temper. The Americans have been wronged. *They have been driven to madness by injustice.* Will you punish them for the madness which you have occasioned? Rather let prudence and temper come first from this side. I will undertake for America that she will follow the example. There are two lines in a ballad of Prior's, of a man's behaviour to his wife, so applicable to you and your colonies, that I cannot help repeating them :—

> ' Be to her faults a little blind ;
> Be to her virtues very kind.'

"Upon the whole, I will beg leave to tell the House what is really my opinion. It is, that the Stamp Act be *repealed absolutely, totally,* and *immediately*. That the reason for the repeal be assigned, because it was founded on an erroneous principle. At the same time, let the sovereign authority of this country over the colonies be asserted in as strong terms as can be devised, and be made to extend to every point of legislation whatsoever. We may bind their *trade*, confine their *manufactures*, and exercise every *power* whatsoever, except that of taking their money out of their pockets without their consent."

The motion for an address was carried without a division. On the 26th of February a bill to repeal the Stamp Act was introduced, and received the Royal assent on the 18th of March. Together with the bill to repeal the Stamp Act was introduced another, called the Declaratory Act, asserting the undoubted power and authority of the King, with the consent of the Lords and Commons in Parliament assembled, to make laws of sufficient force to bind the colonies and people of America in all cases whatsoever. This bill also received the Royal assent on the 18th of March.

This was the first of the great efforts of Pitt to spare his country and the world the evils of the great struggle with the Colonies. The long and vain appeal was to be closed only with his dying speech. But Americans were more ready than his countrymen at home to recognise all they owed him. The Commons House of South Carolina unanimously voted to Pitt a colossal statue in Charleston, "in grateful memory of his services to America"; "for defending the freedom of Americans, the true sons of England, by promoting a Repeal of the Stamp Act in 1766." And the inscription ran :—"Time shall sooner destroy this mark of their esteem than erase from their minds the just sense of his patriotic virtue."

It stands there still, it seems, after all that has passed since that date. "*The right arm was broken off by a British cannon shot in* 1780." Such are the ironies of the whirligig of Time.

CHAPTER IX

THE CHATHAM MINISTRY

THAT second term of responsible office has a fatal and melancholy record. "The Great Commoner" became Earl of Chatham; he was forced to frame a ministry by inevitable pressure of events and the command of the King; whilst disease of body and mind made him powerless, and at last quite irresponsible—ending in mere impotence and the wreck of a great career. He was "lost in quicksands," says Carlyle—"suffering from gout, from semi-insanity." Macaulay attributes his failures to "his distempered state of mind"; and to the "derangement of his faculties" being complete towards the close of his public service. His enthusiastic eulogist mildly describes this as "the least satisfactory part of his history." Indeed it was. The Chatham Ministry is the strange and pathetic story of a Prime Minister continuing in office during two years, though disabled by the state of his mind, not only from directing the policy of his government, but even from seeing his colleagues or knowing what they were doing, whilst an obstinate King and his bewildered servants prepared ruin for the country under the shield of a great name.

The ascendency of Pitt over the minds of politicians and of the public was so great, even whilst he was lying in his sick-room at Bath, that every administration which had not his support, or at least his name, was regarded as a stop-gap. As each of them fell to pieces from internal dissension and their own blunders, the word in public places and in the King's closet had always been, "send for Pitt." By a singular but intelligible coincidence, George, who five years ago was eager to rid himself of Pitt and dreaded him as a tribune of the people, was now as eager to call him to office. Pitt and the King had now the same constitutional aim, different as were the methods they intended to use and the ultimate purpose to be served. It was a large aim : in many ways a necessary and salutary aim: an aim which in effect was practically achieved, even in the lifetime of Pitt and of the King. It was nothing less than the closing the era of government by Magnates.

From the time of William III., government had been in the hands of aristocratic groups, "controlling," as the modern phrase has it, parliamentary influence by means of corruption, patronage, and wealth. The force and sagacity of Walpole had displaced this for a time ; and the genius and popularity of Pitt had shaken it off for a second time. But for six years George III. had found himself in the grip of the great Houses. Their groups were known as their "connection"—Pitt often called them the "factions." He avowed it as his purpose "to get rid of faction." There was a "Pelham faction," a "Bute faction," a "Grenville faction," a "Rockingham faction," a "Bedford faction." And there was Pitt.

George had desired to get free from Pitt in 1761 because Pitt was too masterful, too popular, and George was bent on being a real King himself. But Pitt was now a very different man, both morally and physically, from what he had been in the years of Quebec and Quiberon Bay. George now felt that he could safely use him, that he was the one man living who could break the reign of the Houses and their "connections." George had not the coarseness of his grandfather; he had plenty of bonhomie · and in tactical intrigue· he was a match for any man of his time. His personal treatment of Pitt was, and always remained, gracious, kind, and conciliatory. Pitt, with his magnanimous nature and idealist brain, was over-whelmed by the King's condescension. He overrated his own powers, and above all his influence over men. He again believed that "he could save the country, and that no one else could." His idea was to put an end to government by "connections"; to replace it by government by competent men, chosen without regard to party group or family, supported by the King's confidence and that of the representatives of the people.

It was a fine ideal which in a measure has been realised from time to time ever since Pitt's son came into power. George of course intended to be King himself, when Pitt should have freed him from the confederated Houses. Pitt on his side intended to be master, borrowing the magical authority of the Crown, and counting to regain his old ascendency with the public. If George had been Victoria, if Pitt had possessed the vitality of Palmerston or

Gladstone, this might have been the result. But
George was an artful, obstinate bigot. Pitt was a
physical wreck, hastening to mental impotence. Both
George and Pitt soon found that the lordly Houses
were not to be broken so easily. Both had to appeal
to them, first to one and then to another. Chatham
found that the House of Lords neither followed him
nor feared him; that, when he had quitted it, the
House of Commons became a field for small intrigues
and restless ambitions. And so the Chatham ministry,
after making some well-intentioned attempts at reform,
ended in confusion, and left behind it the seeds of
fatal mischief.

The new ministry was formed, after laborious
negotiations and personal jealousies which we may
now ignore, out of heterogeneous and almost dis-
cordant elements, taken from different parties and even
representing opposing policies. There were some men
of ability, character, and great position, like the young
Duke of Grafton and the young Earl of Shelburne.
Pratt, now Lord Camden, was an able and upright
Chancellor. The honourable General Conway was
drawn off from the Rockingham "connection"; but
Edmund Burke refused to leave it. The brilliant and
unscrupulous Charles Townshend was made Chancellor
of the Exchequer and Leader of the Commons; Lord
North was Paymaster; and Lord Granby was Com-
mander-in-Chief. The "King's friends" held most of
the minor places. Some members of the government
were relicts of the older groups; some differed in
principle from each other and from their chief. None
of them had much experience of affairs, or any political

weight. And the House of Commons was placed in the control of a reckless rhetorician. Not only was the "Cousinhood" now hopelessly broken, but what remained of it was vehemently hostile to Pitt. George Grenville had become his ablest opponent; Lord Temple was reconciled to his brother George, and, with Lyttelton, was in open revolt against his brother-in-law. Pitt pressed on Temple the office of Treasurer, but would not allow him to come in as a sort of Joint Prime Minister. Thereupon the vain Temple went into bitter opposition.

Pitt had grossly miscalculated his own forces when he undertook to frame a government. He strangely underrated the secret powers of the Magnates. And he loftily despised the petty jealousies, vanities, and ambitions of the office-seekers and title-hunters around him. His clear-headed friend, Grafton, said—"his views were great and noble, worthy of a patriot; but they were too visionary." It was not the age of Fabii, Publicolas, and Scipios, but of Newcastle, Townshend, Henry Fox, and Lord Temple. When Pitt went to call on Lord Rockingham, that great personage curtly refused to see him. Temple hired satirists to lampoon his brother-in-law; and Edmund Burke now conceived a vehement prejudice against the man who succeeded and, as he thought, had displaced his own patron, Rockingham.

But more disastrous than the choice of men of different principles or of no principles, was the fatal mistake of transforming the "Great Commoner" into the Earl of Chatham. It was done without the knowledge of his colleagues, causing them dismay,

and rousing the public to indignation. The illumina-
tions were countermanded; the new Bridge was not
to bear his name. The City, it was said, "had
brought in a verdict of *felo de se*." It is probable
that if he had attempted to form his ministry as
Lord Chatham, and not as Mr. Pitt, it would never
have been formed at all. The amazement of the
public, the rage of his party-followers in the City,
was unreasonable and ignorant. In his day—and
ever since, as in our day—a peerage was regarded as
the natural reward of long official service. Peel and
Gladstone are the only examples of Prime Ministers
who, at the end of their careers, have rejected the
honour on principle. William Pitt and Canning died
in office quite young; Melbourne and Palmerston
were Peers. Walpole, Pulteney, Addington, Russell,
Disraeli, all retired late in life to the Upper House.
It was a silly clamour that would have it that Pitt
had "betrayed the people," or had taken a title
as a bribe to change his principles. His whole
after life was a reply to such gross and stupid
calumny.

The reason of the step is plain. Pitt took office at
the urgent and long-continued demand of the King,
full of great things to be done, and fondly believing
himself strong enough to do them. He grossly overrated his moral ascendency. He perhaps overrated
his physical powers. But he was quite aware that
to remain Leader in the Commons, or even to undertake any laborious department, would be his death.
He accordingly took the Privy Seal, a sinecure office,
which usually was held by a Peer. In his eyes,

retirement to the Upper House was an essential condition of his forming a government. His ruined health was the dominant motive. But Pitt, with his superstition about the "grand manner," could see no reason why he should not be created an Earl, any more than Lord John Russell did when he left the Commons as a political compromise. And it would be monstrous injustice to suggest that either statesman forfeited a single principle or forsook any political following when, towards the close of their lives, they sought the solemn peace of the Gilded Chamber.

None the less, the acceptance of the Earldom of Chatham shook Pitt's ascendency to the root, and doomed his second ministry to failure. Though it was in no sense unworthy of him, nor did it at all impair his independence, though in many ways it gave him new wisdom and dignity of bearing, it was a political disaster. It was remembered how Walpole, the Earl of Orford, met in the House of Lords Pulteney, the Earl of Bath, saying, "Here are we, my Lord, the two most insignificant fellows in England." The transfer from the Commons to the Peers was made not at the end of a ministry, but whilst remaining Prime Minister, as was the case with the Earldom of Disraeli. It may have been inevitable. It shows in him a curious *naïveté* of spirit, or it may be an innocent ignorance of the average mind, to have overlooked the consequences of the step. But, if it was inevitable that Pitt should become Lord Chatham —and in some ways perhaps this was a gain to him, a gain to the country,—it would have been better that he should not have formed a Chatham Ministry.

The three keenest observers of that age saw the weakness of the position. Horace Walpole wrote— "That fatal title blasted all the affection which his country had borne to him, and which he had deserved so well." "Lord Chatham's authority ceased with his popularity; and his godhead, when he had affronted his priests." Of the new ministry Walpole wrote with that acute sight and pungent pen which tells us more than Burke's effervescent rhetoric. "The plan will probably be to pick and cull from all quarters, and break all parties as much as possible. From this moment I date the wane of Mr. Pitt's glory; he will want the thorough-bass of drums and trumpets, and is not made for peace." One very bad sign for Lord Chatham is this, wrote Chesterfield: "all his enemies rejoice and all his friends are stupefied and dumb-founded." "He had *fallen upstairs*, and would never stand on his own legs again." What could account for "his going into that *Hospital of Incurables*"? That keen onlooker saw clearly that the opposition in the Commons would prevail, when there was no Pitt to control them. Edmund Burke in a famous passage, more than ordinarily florid and fanciful, described how Lord Chatham "made an administration so chequered and speckled; he put together a piece of joinery so crossly indented and whimsically dovetailed; a Cabinet so variously inlaid; such a piece of diversified mosaic; such a tesselated pavement without cement, here a bit of black stone and there a bit of white; patriots and courtiers; King's friends and Republicans; Whigs and Tories; treacherous friends and open enemies, that it was indeed a very curious show, but utterly unsafe to touch and unsure to stand on."[1]

It was disastrous too that the season of 1766 was the worst on record; the harvest was miserable; riots ensued, and the public effervescence was at its height. Upon this the new ministers laid an embargo on the export of corn, and forbade the distilling of wheat. This, as they knew, was illegal and required confirmation by Parliament. Chatham boldly defended this arbitrary act on the ground of necessity and the needs of the public. It was his first appearance in the House of Lords He spoke with modesty, good sense, and sound law, grounding his defence on the doctrines of Locke. The embargo, he said, was an act of power, *extra vires*—but justified by necessity. The opposition in both Houses was bitter and prolonged. Temple, Lyttelton, Mansfield, the Duke of Bedford, led it in the Lords; George Grenville, Burke, Wedderburn in the Commons. When the Bill of Indemnity was sent up to the Lords from the Commons, Chatham spoke again, and with more vehemence. He said,

---

[1] Here we have Burke in the worst vices of his exuberance. The image is a jumble of tautology, in which rank rhetoric overpowers good sense:—it is literary glitter, not political judgment. It may serve to test the difference between the eloquence of Pitt and that of Burke. Pitt was given to extravagance: but it was the fiery passion of the statesman, not the verbal embroidery of an orator. Chesterfield had already put the truth in simpler words when he wrote: "It is a mosaic ministry made up of *pièces rapportées* from different connections." As a fact, the Chatham ministry contained many honest and capable men, four able statesmen, one very brilliant orator. If Pitt could have remained in the House of Commons, have retained his health and his personal ascendency, the government, which was a ministry of measures, not of parties, nor of Houses, might have done excellent service and have spared us the war with America.

"when the people should condemn him he should tremble; but would set his face against the proudest connection in this country." The Duke of Richmond took this up with heat. "He hoped the nobility would not be brow-beaten by an insolent minister." Chatham hotly replied. The world believed that the Duke had silenced his opponent. The House required both Lords to keep the peace. And as a fact, Chatham did not again appear in the House of Lords during his own administration. It was too true that disease, nervous tension, and an overbearing nature were making Chatham impracticable as a Parliamentary Minister.

There could be no character more hopelessly out of place in forming an administration than Chatham in the crisis of his nervous maladies, unless it were Coriolanus standing for the Consulate. Mr. Pitt had been haughty: but the Earl of Chatham was insolent. He offended the very men he was inviting to join him. When Lord Edgcumbe, the Treasurer of the Household and a strong supporter of his policy, declined to resign, as required, and referred to his own parliamentary interest, Chatham broke out:—"I despise your parliamentary interest! I do not want your assistance—I dare look in the face the proudest connections in this country." After inviting the Duke of Bedford to a friendly conference, he treated him so that his Grace withdrew "in astonishment and angry disgust." General Conway, his Secretary of State, was so deeply offended by Chatham's scornful silence and high-handed proceedings, that he could hardly be induced to retain his seals. He behaved, said Conway, like the Sultan of Constantinople. And, what was perhaps his most unfortunate mistake, Chatham rebuffed Edmund Burke with a coolness which that aspiring orator never forgave. Curiously enough, it was Burke's Free Trade ideas which so deeply offended Chatham's craze for Preferential duties within the Empire. So true is it that ideas of Empire and of Protection go hand in hand! During the first few months of his ministry, whilst Chatham retained some possession of his faculties, his whole remaining energies were taken up with angry altercations, fruitless negotiations, bitter rebuffs, and incessant resignations. It is a pitiful story, for it is the story of disease, of the wreck of a powerful mind and a grand nature under the degeneration of the nervous system.

In such a state of things the policy of government was utterly chaotic; and the House of Commons became the arena of casual intrigues and personal pretensions. And withal there was a strange sense that their real master was in a trance, that there was a head of government somewhere, invisible and inactive as he seemed. This was wonderfully expressed in a famous speech of Burke. "Perhaps this House is not the place where our reasons can be of any avail: the *great person* who is to determine on this question may be a being far above our view; one so immeasurably high, that the greatest abilities (pointing to Mr. Townshend), or the most amiable dispositions that are to be found in this House (pointing to Mr. Conway) may not gain access to him; a being before whom 'thrones, dominations, princedoms, virtues, powers' (waving his hand over the Treasury bench), all veil their faces with their wings. But, though our arguments may not reach him, probably our prayers may !" Burke then apostrophised the Great Minister above, that rules and governs over all, to have mercy and not to destroy the work of his own hands. All this is eloquent—almost poetry—and highly characteristic of two men of genius. It is magnificent invective deriding the mysterious stupor of a great statesman.

Chatham was hardly seated in office before he renewed his old scheme of a vast continental alliance to counterbalance the union of the House of Bourbon in the monarchies of France and Spain. Before taking office he had stipulated for this from the King. His mind was still under the formidable shadow of the Family Compact of 1761. In his first Cabinet Council he passed a minute for forming a Triple Defensive Alliance with Great Britain, Russia, and Prussia as principals, with purport to invite the accession of Denmark, Sweden, and Holland, with such of the German and other powers as could be brought in by mutual agreement.[1] This he described as forming "a firm and solid system in the North to counterbalance the great and formidable alliance framed by the House of Bourbon." Special embassies and instructions were at once sent to St. Petersburg and to Berlin to consolidate the alliance—"to establish a firm and solid system for the maintenance of the public tranquillity," wrote Chatham himself to his ambassador in Berlin. If Frederick would accede to this alliance, "I see before

[1] The insolent and audacious Townshend said, as he left the Council, "Chatham shows us what inferior animals we are ! His superiority is transcendent !"

us," added Chatham, "a happy prospect of durable tranquillity." It seems that Chatham really intended a defensive alliance, and was seriously alarmed at the attitude of France. He evidently considered war to be within measurable calculations.

Was this a mere delusion? Not altogether. The whole force of France and of Spain was now in the hands of men of vigour and ambition. The Bourbon combination was a very real thing, and possessed vast latent resources. The Austrian Empire was now its friend, and incessant secret efforts were made to attach to itself Sweden, Poland, and other powers. Choiseul, a French counterpart of Pitt in his way, was straining every nerve to restore the navy of France, and in four years he accomplished this end whilst he was making secret preparations to strike at England. Choiseul and Chatham distrusted, watched, and feared each other.[1] And it must always be remembered that, only three years after Chatham's death, the triumph of the United States was secured at York Town mainly by the overwhelming superiority of the French fleet in American waters.

---

[1] Lord Edmond Fitzmaurice has collected documentary evidence of all this. He writes (*Life of Shelburne*, ii. 3): "Ever since the peace, Choiseul and Grimaldi had been scheming how to win back what they had lost. They had gained Austria to their alliance; they were intriguing in Stockholm, and plotting in Copenhagen; they were fishing in the troubled waters of Polish politics; their emissaries traversed the English colonies; their spies surveyed the defences of the English coast; Portsmouth was to be destroyed, and Gibraltar to be seized by a *coup de main*; Avignon was to be annexed to France, and Portugal to Spain; Corsica was to be invaded; Geneva was threatened." The two ministers resolved to wait. "Their only fear was lest Chatham should precipitate hostilities."

But if there was real ground for guarding against the designs of the Bourbon monarchies to retaliate upon the power which had crushed and despoiled them, there is no answer to the admirable wisdom of Frederick in declining to enter a new coalition. Russia was now on more friendly terms with him than she was with England. She thought a Prussian alliance quite sufficient support, as it certainly was. In reply to the proposed triple alliance, Frederick said he now saw no likelihood of war. France, in her exhausted state, could not make war; Spain even less, owing to her internal troubles. Such a confederation as was proposed would give jealousy to other powers, and afford a pretext for disturbing the general tranquillity. Alliances made with a view to distant events "are matters of ostentation." The Italians had a proverb—*Chi sta bene non se muove, i.e.* "Leave well alone."

The Prussian King added that he feared the many questions outstanding between England and France would be the occasion of a new war between them, in which Prussia would have no interest to engage. He was now determined to devote himself to the peaceful organisation of his own kingdom, and to restore the sacrifices made in the late war. He could not forget the way in which he had been treated when England hurried on a peace without considering the interests of her Prussian ally. The peace had been followed by a series of weak and shifting governments in England. And, much as he respected his friend who had now succeeded to power, he feared that, in becoming Earl of Chatham, Mr. Pitt had greatly injured the power he used to wield. Here as elsewhere, one is

impressed with the truth that Frederick II. as a
statesman was far the greatest man of the eighteenth
century.

Another grand scheme on which Chatham's mind
was now bent was the future settlement of the new
Empire in India. A vast territory larger than the
British Islands, with a population of twenty millions
and a revenue of five or six millions a year, was now
held by a trading company, whose dominant ideas
were plunder and dividends. Their officials were
insubordinate and rapacious, and the conquered subjects were the victims of every form of misrule and
extortion. At home the proprietors cared for nothing
but to increase the dividends, which they intended to
fix by a guarantee of ten years at fifteen per cent. on
their holdings. This system of irresponsible iniquity
Chatham resolved to close. And the first step was to
bring the conquered lands under the control of the
Crown, and to make a parliamentary settlement of
revenues which the tradesmen claimed as their private
perquisite.

In letters to his colleagues Chatham speaks of "the
transcendent object, East India affairs," "the greatest
of all objects"—the question as to the right of the
Company to dispose of this enormous revenue. His
view of the right was this, as he explained long afterwards :—There was a mixed right to the territorial
revenues of the conquered provinces between the
State and the Company—the State being entitled to
the larger share as the larger contributor by its fleet
and men. And the Company's share could never be
considered as private property to be divided as profits,

but must be held in trust for the public purposes of defence of India and the extension of trade. He held that conquests of vast territories, never contemplated by the Company's charter and mainly made by the forces of the Crown, could confer no indefeasible rights of sovereignty on a body of traders. These noble provinces must be claimed as dominions of the Crown, and governed as such. The Charter had only secured to the Company a few factories on the rivers and coasts, but not such vast provinces as Bengal, Orissa, and Behar. The merchants were entitled to their commercial privileges and a moderate return for their invested capital.

So far Chatham's statesmanlike insight has been amply justified by events. But his eager ambition saw visions of an era of just and beneficent government dispensed to the people of India; and, in place of "enriching a band of greedy factors," a revenue which should eventually lighten the taxation of our country, and extinguish the debt which had been created by the wars. In this his anticipations egregiously outran the facts. Like the rest of his contemporaries, he greatly overrated the wealth of Hindustan. And he wholly failed to gauge the narrow and self-seeking spirits by whom he was served and surrounded. In the result something was effected, but his noble hopes of reforming the government of India were destroyed by the intrigues of his colleagues and the breakdown of his own powers.

Chatham's first aim was to obtain a searching inquiry in Parliament; and for this purpose he put up his friend, Alderman Beckford, to move for this as an

independent member of the House of Commons. Chatham himself declined to formulate any scheme of reform until the inquiry was complete, nor would he even submit a scheme to his Cabinet. There was nothing in this course unusual in such cases of complicated legislation. The inquiry was warmly opposed in successive debates by the Opposition leaders, who defended the Company in the name of their Charter. It is one of the ironies of history that the most eloquent speech in resisting any restraint on the arbitrary powers of the Company was delivered by Edmund Burke. He made one of his most brilliant orations in defence of the colleagues and patrons of Clive and Hastings—a speech wherein occurred the Apocalyptic attack on Chatham already cited. Had Chatham succeeded in reorganising the government of India in 1766, Burke would not have had to denounce such a record of crimes and tyranny as he unfolded at Westminster in 1788.

When the inquiry came before the House, and during the debates, Chatham was in his sick-room, either at Marlborough, Hampstead, or at Bath, occasionally dictating peremptory letters to Grafton and Shelburne, but attending no Councils nor appearing in Parliament. Conway, whom he had deeply offended, and Townshend, the brilliant mountebank, whom he had so unwisely placed in the Exchequer, both played false to their paralysed chief and thwarted any serious inquiry. Chatham (by correspondence) thundered against the weakness and disloyalty of his colleagues, reiterated, with his usual vehemence, his anxieties, his fears, and his behests. Some check was put on the

division of the spoil. But nothing effective came of
it; and for a generation India remained the happy
hunting-ground of British "nabobs."

Another urgent reform attempted by the Chatham
ministry was to remedy the gross misgovernment of
Ireland. The rule of that kingdom was a corrupt
oligarchy, controlled by Lords Justices, with little interference from the central government, and a Parliament
of borough-mongers, elected for the life of the King.
In 1767 Lord Townshend was sent over by Chatham
as Viceroy, with instructions to remain in constant
residence, virtually superseding the irresponsible power
of the Lords Justices. The new ministry were prepared to support a Septennial Act to limit the duration
of the Irish Parliament, to reform the tenure of the
Judges on the English basis, of holding office "during
good conduct" and not "during pleasure" of the
Crown. The whole conduct of Pitt, as of Chatham,
whether in his two ministries as well as before and
after both of them, was to extend towards Ireland the
same spirit of liberal government, the same respect
for local liberties and popular representation which
he advocated towards the Colonies. But the utter
collapse of his health prevented Chatham during his
second administration from carrying through any
effective reform—just as it had done in the case of the
government of India.

The next escapade of the unscrupulous rhetorician
to whom Chatham had entrusted the finances of the
country was to allow the Opposition to reduce the
land tax from four to three shillings in the pound. By
this blunder the Exchequer lost half a million, the

amount, as Chesterfield said, "of the bribe the landed gentlemen had voted to themselves." Chatham was incensed with Townshend for this and for his conduct in the India question, and wrote that he or the Chancellor of the Exchequer must quit office. He would have acted on this threat, but now he fell into such a state of nervous prostration that he declined to take part in any business, or even to have matters of business referred to him at all.

In the meantime Charles Townshend broke out into an act of reckless folly, far more serious than any of his previous extravagances. Without consulting his colleagues, he proposed an import duty on various goods entering America. To this the Cabinet objected; but, in the absence of Chatham, unable even to consult him, to resist Townshend, or to dismiss him, the ministers accepted the measure, which quietly passed both Houses. The ignorance of the times and the arrogant complacency of the home government were such that this critical step passed without opposition and with little remark. It was the beginning of the long and ruinous struggle which for twenty years divided the mother country and her American colonies.

The Duke of Grafton, Chatham's most trusted friend, quotes the Earl's letter to himself (March 1767), to the effect that "the East India business was the capital object of the publick upon which Lord Chatham would stand or fall." He then tells us how "a suppressed gout falling on his nerves, to a degree sufficient to master his resolution," rendered Chatham unfit to see any of his colleagues. "From this time he became invisible." "Here, in fact, was the end of

his administration." The Duke and the Chancellor went to the King and told him that the ministry was in fact dissolved, and they urged George to call upon Chatham to advise him as to his course. All that they got was a statement in Lady Chatham's handwriting declining any visit. The King wrote within the month of June no less than eight letters to his Prime Minister urging on him the chaos into which government had fallen, imploring him to see the Duke or to give some suggestion as to what should be done. To every appeal came the same reply. He is overwhelmed with the boundless extent of the royal goodness. He lays himself at the King's feet. In his extreme weakness of nerves and spirits he "could not sustain the weight of an audience": he could not offer any suggestion; he is utterly incapable of the smallest effort.

The Duke did obtain one interview with Chatham, and he reports: "His nerves and spirits were affected to a dreadful degree: and the sight of his great mind bowed down, and thus weakened by disorder, would have filled me with grief and concern, even if I had not borne a sincere attachment to his person and character." It appeared, he says, like cruelty to have to put a man he valued to so great suffering. All that the Duke could wring from his shattered chief was a request to remain in office and to open negotiations with the Bedfords rather than the Rockinghams— advice truly unfortunate, to be explained only by aberration of mind. At this time his condition is thus described by the secretary of George Grenville as "the lowest dejection and debility that mind or body can be in." He sits all day leaning on his hands which

rested on a table : would permit no one to remain in his
room, knocks when he needs anything and then silently
signals to the attendant to retire. At the mention of
politics he starts and trembles violently from head to
foot. He could bear no noise, and his children had to
be removed from his roof. To avoid sound, he took
house after house near his own. He ordered plantations to be made round his garden at ruinous cost and
hurried on with feverish haste by night as by day.
His appetite was sickly and uncertain. He could bear
no delay ; and kept chickens ready cooked at any hour
that he felt able to eat. By a deed he gave Lady
Chatham a power of attorney to transact all business
of every kind. He moved from Hampstead to
Somersetshire, and then to Bath. He passionately
sought to repurchase Hayes Place, which he had sold
to Mr. Thomas Walpole. "That might have saved
me !" he murmured, when the purchaser hesitated to
part with his bargain. But at Lady Chatham's earnest
entreaty, Walpole reluctantly consented to surrender
the place.

Such was the pitiable nervous prostration of the
"great Earl," in which the Chatham administration
fell to pieces, whilst the seeds of future disaster were
sown thick in the confusion of parties and the tangle
of folly, intrigue, and obstinacy in which politics were
plunged. It was natural that spiteful and scandalous
reports were rife in the world. Some said he was
mad : others, that he was shamming madness. Even
Horace Walpole allowed his ill-nature so far to over
come his good sense as to put it on record that he
inclined to think his extravagances were feigned. The

lampoons were continual, and the pseudo-Junius called him "a lunatic brandishing a crutch." He could no longer "lie on his back and talk fustian," as Burke said. He was not at all insane : still less was he acting a part. He was afflicted with nervous paralysis, and sat impotent and silent. And the fortunes of England were delivered over to the perverse ambition of a dogged King, to the mischievous counsels of a distracted ministry, whilst the greatest brain and the finest soul of the age lay as it were in some mysterious trance.[1]

---

[1] Lord Edmond Fitzmaurice, when preparing his *Life of Shelburne*, obtained from Sir Andrew Clark an opinion as to Chatham's complaint. "Suppressed gout disordered the whole nervous system, and drove him into a state of mental depression, varying with excitement and equivalent to insanity. But there was no specific brain disease." After a bad attack of external gout the patient entirely recovered his force of mind.

CHAPTER X

DEFENCE OF IRELAND AND INDIA

THE remaining years of Chatham's life, from his final
resignation of office in October 1768, until his death in
May 1778, were broken by long intervals of retirement
and disease, but were illuminated by some splendid
efforts from time to time to withstand the follies and
crimes of those in power, to call out the moral sense of
his countrymen, to give voice to the inmost warning
of conscience, of reason, and justice. He warmly
defended the freedom and independence of the Parliament of Ireland. He passionately called for reformation of the corrupt government of India, such as might
win the confidence and affections of the native
population. He constantly pressed for a Reform of
Parliament and the amendment of the system of close
Boroughs. He was regarded as the champion of the
Protestant Dissenters against the prejudices and ex-
clusions of a pampered Establishment. He warned the
nation of the danger of allowing the strength of the
Navy to be reduced, a warning the force of which was
so soon to be justified at York Town But the main
strength of his efforts in public and in private was
given all through these years to the struggle with the

American Colonies. By speeches in the House of
Lords, by appeals to influential men, in conferences
with Dr. Franklin, in many personal negotiations, he
strove to stem the oppressive policy of the King, and to
satisfy the just claims of the American States. He
inveighed, with horror and with a magnificence of
language which has grown to be a part of English
literature, against the perverse folly of prolonging a
hopeless and disastrous Civil War, and against the
inhuman barbarities that too often disgraced it.

The course of time, the slow advance of justice and
morality in matters of State, have justified every one
of these warnings and appeals. Chatham was the
precursor in fact of reforms which were not achieved
until the century which followed his own : which even
yet have been but imperfectly effected : some of
which are burning problems with us still to-day. It is
to be numbered amongst the heaviest clouds which
darken the history of our country, that these splendid
attempts of the fallen statesman were heard by the
King and his creatures with sullen disdain. Not one
of them had any effect in changing the course of events
or in mitigating the disasters and humiliations which
criminal folly entailed on its authors. But whilst
these noble words of the lonely statesman are enshrined
in the records of our country, he will not be to future
generations that which he was to his own—a voice
crying in the wilderness. In the eyes of those who
place Honour and Justice above Empire, who place the
Happiness of the People above Glory and Conquests,
the last ten years of Chatham's career, though he
laboured in vain to convince a besotted faction, and to

reverse a policy of ruin, will always stand forth with a truer brilliance than the five years of his dictatorship when he sent forth fleets to annihilate those of our rivals, and organised the armies which conquered an Empire.

The state of his health, his irritable and domineering temper, the angry air of suspicion and jealousy in the competing factions amongst whom he lived, whose suspicions he so deeply imbibed, rendered this period of Chatham's life a melancholy failure. Had he been born to the throne of an hereditary despot, as were King Frederick and the Emperor Joseph, had his mind not been unhinged by disease, and his nature not soured by the enmity of weak men born into great power, Chatham would have proved one of the most triumphant rulers of modern times. If he had possessed the adroitness of Walpole, the serene wisdom of Washington, the patience and knowledge of the world of his own son, he might have again commanded the country. But never was man less patient, less tolerant of weakness, more disdainful of all the arts of compromise and conciliation. If only he could have formed a genuine and permanent alliance with Rockingham, Camden, Shelburne, and Burke, from the hour when he recovered command of his powers; if only, with all his devotion to the Constitution, he could have conceived the position of a Constitutional Minister; if, once the idol of the people, he could have remained in the House of Commons, and could have carried through its Reform—then our country might have been saved from some of its worst excesses in India, in Ireland, and at home, and from some of its

bitterest humiliations in America. But what Horace
Walpole called his "presumptuous impracticability"
made such a coalition impossible from the first.

When, in January 1767, Chatham was attacked with
gout and retired to Bath, his colleagues never saw him
again; and the confusion was unexampled in modern
history. As Burke said long afterwards—"when his
face was hid but for a moment, his whole system was
on a wide sea, without chart or compass." His colleagues never presumed to have an opinion of their
own. They were whirled about, the sport of every
gust. They turned the vessel wholly out of the course
of his policy. It was thus that, using his name, they
proceeded to tax America. Lord Charlemont wrote
(9th April)—"Charles Townshend is at open war,
Conway is angry, Lord Shelburne out of humour, and
the Duke of Grafton by no means pleased. The ministry
is divided into as many parties as there are men in it."

All this time George kept writing friendly letters
to Chatham, insisting on his remaining in office—
"though confined to your house, your name has been
sufficient to enable *my* administration to proceed. I,
therefore, in the most earnest manner, call on you to
continue in your employment" (the King to Chatham,
January 23, 1768). George could easily afford to be
gracious. He obtained the great name of the Earl,
who could do nothing, who knew nothing. In the
meantime, the King was having his own way, and
carrying on what he naively called "his administration."

In the month of January 1768 a wretched job
made it necessary to set the Privy Seal to an appoint-

"England, it is evident, profits by drai... vast incomes spent here from that countr... as an English peer, advise the King on... accidental English policy, to reject a... over here, as the genuine desire of th... acting in their proper and peculiar sp... inherent, exclusive right, by raising su... think best. This great principle of t... mental, and with me so sacred... outweighs all other consideration...

Lord Rockingham oppo...
Shelburne to join him in...
And Edmund Burke. Here a second...
Absentee Tax. Here a... defending... of the soil. As...
resisting, and Chatham's attempt to check the abuses o...
interest of the poor cultivators. The correspon-
had opposed Chatham's... so we find him opposed to Chatham.
Indian "nabobs," so we... Shelburne very honourably of Chatham.
view as to taxing the Irish absentees... admitted that all his
dence continued; and Shelburne and generosity of Chatham, for
way to the superior wisdom... Chatham admitted that all his
In a second letter, Chatham... with Irish landowners. Never-
personal prejudices were... considerable estates.
two of his relations held...

theless, he continues:—

"The fitness or justice of the tax in question, I shall not consider, if the Commons of Ireland send it here." . . . "The line of the Constitution—a line written in the broadest letter, through every page of the history of Parliament and people—tells me, that the Commons are to judge of the purse in the expediency of supplies." "This Power of the purse in the Commons is fundamental and inherent; to translate it from them to the King in Council, is to annihilate Parliament."

In result, the landowners succeeded in having the

ment. As Chatham was incapable even of this effort, three private persons were named commissioners to act for six weeks. The King and his ministers would not let their victim go. For months things stagnated and went to chaos, Lady Chatham answering all appeals and refusing all interviews. At last, in October 1768, a letter in her handwriting was sent to the Duke of Grafton begging him to obtain the King's permission to resign the Privy Seal. The Duke hesitated and pressed the Earl to remain. The King, almost losing his temper, wrote directly to Lord Chatham—"I think I have a right to *insist* on your remaining in my service." An abject letter, in her ladyship's hand—a letter which a Grand Vizier might have sent to Sultan Amurath—(October 14) finally closed this melancholy episode, and brought to an end the Chatham ministry. It had lasted nominally two years and two months. It had at last found strength enough to insist on dying.

The appearance of Chatham on the political field in the last years of his life was so irregular and spasmodic, had so little practical effect on legislation and government, and was itself so seldom continuous, that it would be inconvenient to record it in chronological order. It must be grouped under a few distinct subjects; and it will be best to collect his utterances and schemes under the following heads: (1) the good government of Ireland, of India, and other parts of the Empire; (2) Constitutional questions and the function of Parliament; (3) the quarrel with the American Colonies, and the formation of the United States.

With regard to Ireland, the administration of which

Bill thrown out in the Irish Parliament; and the perilous resort to King George's fiat was not required. But the letters display how intensely Chatham held by his doctrine that the taxes of the Irish people could only be voted by their own representatives—in their own Parliament.

The critical question of the independence of the National Parliament of Ireland was not decided until long after Chatham's time. But, whatever doubts he may have once had, he repeatedly declared himself to his colleague, Lord Shelburne, as opposed to the legislative Union of the Irish and British Parliaments, on the ground of the bad effect it would have on the English Parliament. This Lord Shelburne communicated to Arthur Young. The Irish Speaker, when resisting the Union in February 1800, repeated that Lord Chatham had always objected to the Union, lest the additional members from Ireland might alter the constitution of the House. It is clear that the people of Ireland had felt at least as much enthusiasm for the Liberal Statesman as did the people of Scotland and of England. The merchants and traders of Dublin had presented him with an address of admiration on his retirement from office. And the citizens of Cork had placed a marble statue of him in their Exchange.

During Chatham's own ministry, the urgent need of reform in the government of India was ever in his mind. He wrote from Bath to Lord Shelburne (January 1767) about "the transcendent object which possesses my mind, the East India business." But in his absence, in spite of constant exchange of letters with Shelburne and Townshend, nothing effective

Iro...
Irish Parl...
a Habeas Corp...
ances of the monstrou...
consistently Chatham's pr...
genuine Irish government, to ma...
ment solely responsible for Irish tax...
require from the Lord-Lieutenant continuous ...
in Dublin. The collapse of Chatham's health, and ...
disorganisation into which this threw his colleagues, had prevented any of these urgent reforms being carried through.

Although Chatham never at any time was able to effect any reform in Ireland, we are not left in doubt about the principles which he maintained. The very remarkable correspondence between him and Lord Shelburne, in October 1773, fully explains his views. In that year it was proposed to put a tax of two shillings in the pound on the net annual profits of all land-owners in Ireland *who should not actually reside in the Kingdom for six months in each year.* It was hotly urged by the English party both there and in Britain that any such Bill, if carried in the Irish Parliament, should be annulled by the Crown. Lord Shelburne, whose family held great Irish estates, consulted Chatham as to the course to be pursued. Chatham's answer was emphatic—against any interference from England. This proposal, he said, however severe against absentees, is founded in strong Irish policy, to compel more of the product of Irish estates to be spent in Ireland, and not here.

could be done. In February the Duke of Grafton wrote with an account of a meeting of ministers, "they were most thoroughly convinced that his presence was absolutely necessary to give dignity to the administration and to carry through this affair (the most important of all) of the East India Company, in which they all think that there is no stirring without your assistance and concurrence." And the Duke frankly adds that he is ready to join in any plan which approved itself to the great experience and ability of his chief. But nothing beyond abortive attempts came from this headless administration.

For years, as we know, abortive attempts were made to solve the problem of Indian Government, a problem which wrecked one minister after another. Lord Chatham does not seem to have spoken in the House on these questions; but in letters to his colleagues from time to time we find what his views and advice had been. Colonel Barré, who had now become his friend and warm supporter, asked Chatham's opinion as to the Bill promoted by the East India Company to enable them to raise further military forces (February 1771). Other friends asked for his views. Chatham replies (21st February 1771) :—

"As to the East India Company's Bill for recruiting, I disapprove it absolutely. I have seen regalities taken away by Act of Parliament; and shall not concur in an Act to attribute sovereign power in England to Leadenhall Street. I think the attempt daring, and the power preposterous: out of all line of the Constitution."

When, in 1772 and 1773, public opinion forced the government of Lord North to carry through the India

Acts designed to stop the worst enormities of the Company's Raj and to transfer their irresponsible power to a body representing the State at home, Chatham was unable to take part in debate, but we find him at every point warmly supporting the Reforms. The Report of the Secret Committee of December 1772, on which the government action was based, met with Chatham's hearty approval:—

"I am much edified with it. As far as it has gone, I like the spirit of it well; as it does 'nothing extenuate, nor set down aught in malice.'

"*Trade in India, internal and external, stands at present on little else than the guns of our ships and fortresses: a forced foundation which will fail, if not timely strengthened by a system of justice and humanity, of sounder and larger policy.*"

When the Acts of 1773 came on for debate, Chatham from his retreat in Somersetshire warmly applauded the efforts of Colonel Barré, who took the lead in arguing the case with what, Chatham writes to Shelburne, was a "noble and universally applauded speech on India." The case of the Company and their "vested interests" in extortion, oppression, and fraud, was maintained by Edmund Burke, who took the lead on the side of opposition. Strange destiny, which for the third time found Burke the passionate advocate of Property and Reaction, whilst Chatham was a stout champion of the People and of Reform! There was some strange antipathy between these two men—the finest brains and natures of their time. Both were high-minded, profound in insight, generous, with passionate imagination. Burke was a philosopher, a man of letters, an idealist, and a born Conservative. Chatham was a man of action with a genius for efficiency, a popular tribune, but a born ruler of men.

In May 1773, Chatham again pressed on Shelburne that "Indian affairs are in a most interesting crisis; nor can any public object be more important to the honour and welfare of the nation." The government, with a majority in both Houses, were carrying their Bill to limit the irresponsible liberty of the Company, whose vested interests under charter were being passionately defended by the Rockingham party and the "nabob" ring. As to the claim of the Company to the entire revenue that could be squeezed out of the natives, Chatham writes :—

"Dividends are in their nature strictly limited to the profits of trade ; anything more is undue, and an imposition and defrauding of the public services. Inland trade exclusive of the natives is the rankest and most odious oppression to be abolished for ever. This, together with the want of justice in judicature, has lost us the favourable dispositions of Hindostan. Justice should be solidly established under independent judges, holding their offices as the judges here, removable only by Address of Parliament, and under severest penalties if they meddle in trade."

This was directed against the monstrous system under which the officials of the Company claimed complete monopoly of the inland trade of the Peninsula, fixing themselves the prices at which they chose both to buy and sell.

Well might Lord Shelburne write to Chatham that "the crimes and frauds of the servants in India, enormous as they appear in the Reports, are not yet fully stated. The Directors, occupied in domestic

pursuits equally fraudulent, have produced the effect
of accomplices throughout; while the proprietors
who, as the last resort, ought to be the purest to the
objects of their charter, appear the most servile instruments of both." To this Chatham replies:—

"India teems with iniquities so rank, as to smell to
heaven and earth. The reformation of them, if pursued in
a pure spirit of justice, might exalt the nation, and endear
the English name throughout the world; but the generous
purpose is no sooner conceived in the hearts of the few, but
by-ends and sinister interests taint the execution, and power
is grasped at, where redress should be the only object.

"The putting under circumscription and control the high
and dangerous prerogatives of war and alliances, so abused
in India, I cannot but approve, as it shuts the door against
insatiable rapine and detestable enormities, as have, on
some occasions, stained the English name, and disgraced
human nature. I approve, too, of the nomination of judges
by the Crown; but as they are to hold their offices during
pleasure, I cannot consider them as judges, but as dependent
instruments of power.

"The abolition of inland trade on private accounts is
highly laudable, as far as that provision goes; but I would
assuredly carry the prohibition further, and open again to
the natives and other Eastern merchants the inland trade
of Bengal, and abolish all monopolies on the Company's
account; which now operate to the unjust exclusion of an
oppressed people, and to the impoverishing and alienating
of these extensive and populous provinces. *The hearts and
good affections of Bengal are of more worth than all the profits
of ruinous and odious monopolies.*"

In the summer of 1769, the town was startled, and
all the political quidnuncs were set in motion by the
unexpected appearance of Chatham at the King's
Levee, and an interview between them afterwards in
the closet. It had come about in this way. In the

autumn of the preceding year, Chatham had another
severe attack of gout, and a second in the following
spring. This seemed to clear his brain and restore
his nerves. He became reconciled to Lord Temple,
who visited him at Hayes, and effusively had the visit
recorded as "a most cordial, firm, and perpetual union,
to which Mr. Grenville has heartily acceded." The
invalid had shaken off his gloom, and after two years
and a half, he not only came up to London, but he
attended the Levee. The circumstance must be told
in the inimitable language of Horace Walpole.

"Lord Chatham appeared at the King's Levée when
it was thought he would never produce himself again,
or was not fit to be produced in public. He was
perfectly well, and had grown fat. The Duke of
Grafton had just time to apprise the King of this
mysterious visit. The King was very gracious, and
whispered him to come into the closet after the levée,
which he did, and stayed there twenty minutes."
And then the lively diarist pours forth the gossip of
the day with all its suspicions and rumours. Had the
ex-minister, who seemed to have risen from the dead
to overthrow all the combinations of the day, and
to make new, come to consult with the King about
the Middlesex election of Wilkes, or had he come to
claim power for himself? Had he been sent for, or
did he come up of his own accord? Why was he so
cold to the Duke of Grafton and the Duke of Bedford?
Why so friendly to Lord Granby and General Harvey?
And was Lord Temple in the game? and so forth, as
Chatham lingered after the audience, as if to convince
the Court that he had recovered his health and under-
standing.

He had indeed fluttered the Volscians at St. James's.
Lord Mansfield had hoped the ministry could hold on,
"if that madman Chatham did not come to throw a
fire-ball amongst them." Had he thrown it? Burke
wondered if he had only come to talk some "creeping,
explanatory, ambiguous matter in the true Chathamic
style." Explanatory perhaps; but was Chatham often
ambiguous, was he ever *creeping*? As a matter of fact,
Chatham now felt himself restored to health and life,
and resolved to show the King and the world that
he was. We now know exactly what had been
Chatham's purpose, and what he said. Nothing could
be simpler and more straightforward. The Duke of
Grafton wrote a minute at the time of what had
passed, evidently from the King's own words.

George was gracious, regretted that illness had
caused the Earl's resignation. Chatham replied that
he could not continue to serve when unable to approve
what he thought good, or dissent from what he thought
bad. He thought this recent case (Wilkes's) had been
mismanaged. It ought to have been treated with
contempt from the first. And he was not satisfied
with what had been done as to Indian government,
and the powers left with the Company. He did not
think his health would ever allow him again to attend
in Parliament. If it did, and he should dissent from
any measure proposed, he hoped his Majesty would
believe that it did not arise from any personal consideration, as he had not a tittle to find fault with
in the conduct of any individual. "His Majesty
might be assured that it could not arise from ambition,
as he felt so strongly the weak state from which he

ment.   As Chatham was incapable even of this effort, three private persons were named commissioners to act for six weeks.   The King and his ministers would not let their victim go.   For months things stagnated and went to chaos, Lady Chatham answering all appeals and refusing all interviews.   At last, in October 1768, a letter in her handwriting was sent to the Duke of Grafton begging him to obtain the King's permission to resign the Privy Seal.   The Duke hesitated and pressed the Earl to remain.   The King, almost losing his temper, wrote directly to Lord Chatham—"I think I have a right to *insist* on your remaining in my service." An abject letter, in her ladyship's hand—a letter which a Grand Vizier might have sent to Sultan Amurath— (October 14) finally closed this melancholy episode, and brought to an end the Chatham ministry.   It had lasted nominally two years and two months.   It had at last found strength enough to insist on dying.

The appearance of Chatham on the political field in the last years of his life was so irregular and spasmodic, had so little practical effect on legislation and government, and was itself so seldom continuous, that it would be inconvenient to record it in chronological order.   It must be grouped under a few distinct subjects; and it will be best to collect his utterances and schemes under the following heads: (1) the good government of Ireland, of India, and other parts of the Empire; (2) Constitutional questions and the function of Parliament; (3) the quarrel with the American Colonies, and the formation of the United States.

With regard to Ireland, the administration of which

Chatham was the nominal head had started in July 1766 with excellent intentions:—the reform of the Irish Parliament, the independence of the Irish Judges, a Habeas Corpus Act, and the abolition of the grievances of the monstrous Pension list. In short, it was consistently Chatham's principle to give Ireland a genuine Irish government, to make the Irish Parliament solely responsible for Irish taxation, and to require from the Lord-Lieutenant continuous residence in Dublin. The collapse of Chatham's health, and the disorganisation into which this threw his colleagues, had prevented any of these urgent reforms being carried through.

Although Chatham never at any time was able to effect any reform in Ireland, we are not left in doubt about the principles which he maintained. The very remarkable correspondence between him and Lord Shelburne, in October 1773, fully explains his views. In that year it was proposed to put a tax of two shillings in the pound on the net annual profits of all landowners in Ireland *who should not actually reside in the Kingdom for six months in each year.* It was hotly urged by the English party both there and in Britain that any such Bill, if carried in the Irish Parliament, should be annulled by the Crown. Lord Shelburne, whose family held great Irish estates, consulted Chatham as to the course to be pursued. Chatham's answer was emphatic—against any interference from England. This proposal, he said, however severe against absentees, is founded in strong Irish policy, to compel more of the product of Irish estates to be spent in Ireland, and not here.

"England, it is evident, profits by draining Ireland of the vast incomes spent here from that country. But I could not, as an English peer, advise the King on principles of indirect, accidental English policy, to reject a tax on absentees, sent over here, *as the genuine desire of the Commons of Ireland, acting in their proper and peculiar sphere, and exercising their inherent, exclusive right, by raising supplies in the manner they think best.* This great principle of the Constitution is so fundamental, and with me so sacred and indispensable, that it outweighs all other considerations."

Lord Rockingham opposed all this, and pressed Shelburne to join him in having the Bill disallowed. And Edmund Burke vehemently denounced the Absentee Tax. Here a second time we find Burke resisting, and Chatham defending, a reform in the interest of the poor cultivators of the soil. As Burke had opposed Chatham's attempt to check the abuses of Indian "nabobs," so we find him opposed to Chatham's view as to taxing the Irish absentees. The correspondence continued; and Shelburne very honourably gave way to the superior wisdom and generosity of Chatham. In a second letter, Chatham admitted that all his personal prejudices were with Irish landowners, for two of his relations held considerable estates. Nevertheless, he continues :—

"The fitness or justice of the tax in question, I shall not consider, if the Commons of Ireland send it here." . . . "The line of the Constitution—a line written in the broadest letter, through every page of the history of parliament and people— tells me, that the Commons are to judge of the propriety and expediency of supplies." "This power of the purse in the Commons is fundamental and inherent; to translate it from them to the King in Council, is to annihilate Parliament."

In result, the landowners succeeded in having the

Bill thrown out in the Irish Parliament; and the perilous resort to King George's fiat was not required. But the letters display how intensely Chatham held by his doctrine that the taxes of the Irish people could only be voted by their own representatives—in their own Parliament.

The critical question of the independence of the National Parliament of Ireland was not decided until long after Chatham's time. But, whatever doubts he may have once had, he repeatedly declared himself to his colleague, Lord Shelburne, as opposed to the legislative Union of the Irish and British Parliaments, on the ground of the bad effect it would have on the English Parliament. This Lord Shelburne communicated to Arthur Young. The Irish Speaker, when resisting the Union in February 1800, repeated that Lord Chatham had always objected to the Union, lest the additional members from Ireland might alter the constitution of the House. It is clear that the people of Ireland had felt at least as much enthusiasm for the Liberal Statesman as did the people of Scotland and of England. The merchants and traders of Dublin had presented him with an address of admiration on his retirement from office. And the citizens of Cork had placed a marble statue of him in their Exchange.

During Chatham's own ministry, the urgent need of reform in the government of India was ever in his mind. He wrote from Bath to Lord Shelburne (January 1767) about "the transcendent object which possesses my mind, the East India business." But in his absence, in spite of constant exchange of letters with Shelburne and Townshend, nothing effective

was recovering, and which might daily threaten him, that office therefore of any sort could no longer be desirable to him."

From this hour Chatham neither held nor sought any office, nor did he ever see the King again. The history of England might have been different, if George could have honestly trusted the sincere words in which his proud servant took his last farewell.

CHAPTER XI

DEFENCE OF THE CONSTITUTION

CHATHAM was by fixed principle a Whig of the old school, a firm believer in the Settlement of 1689, albeit alien to any particular Whig "connection." His whole conception of politics was the efficient rule of a trained statesman, implicitly trusted by a free Parliament. Thus it came about that, when not in power himself, he was in continual opposition to forces which he scorned, but could not control—a venal and servile House of Commons; a House of Peers divided into rival "factions"; a King and his Court, successfully intriguing so as to manipulate both. Chatham's splendid efforts to bridle Prerogative, to guide Parliament, and to stir the conscience of the nation, met with no success, but they left a great inheritance to those who came after him.

On the first occasion of his return to Parliament, Chatham poured out his passionate sense of constitutional right with even more than his usual violence of language.

"My Lords, I need not look abroad for grievances. The great capital mischief is fixed at home. It corrupts the very foundation of our political existence, and preys upon the

206

vitals of the State. The Constitution at this moment stands violated. Until that wound be healed, until the grievance be redressed, it is in vain to recommend union to Parliament, in vain to promote concord among the people. If we mean seriously to unite the nation within itself, we must convince them that their complaints are regarded, that their injuries shall be redressed. On that foundation, I would take the lead in recommending peace and harmony to the people. On any other, I would never wish to see them united again. If the breach in the constitution be effectually repaired, the people will of themselves return to a state of tranquillity. If not— may discord prevail for ever ! "

The orator went on, apparently losing control of his tongue, to the effect that if the King's servants would not permit a constitutional question to be decided by the principles of the Constitution, then, old as he was, he hoped to see the issue fairly tried between the people and the government. When the liberty of the subject was invaded, without redress, resistance was justified. "The Constitution has its political Bible, by which, if it be fairly consulted, every political question may, and ought to be determined. Magna Charta, the Petition of Rights, and the Bill of Rights, form that code which I call *The Bible of the English Constitution*. Had some of his Majesty's unhappy predecessors trusted less to the comments of their ministers, had they been better read in the text itself, the glorious Revolution would have remained only possible in theory, and would not now have existed upon record, a formidable example to their successors." If Walpole said truly, "it was not his style to be harsh in the closet," his style was outspoken enough in the Lords.

In the same speech Chatham went on to expound

his view of a Reform of Parliament. The boroughs, he said, had been called the rotten parts of the Constitution. Corrupt as they are, they must be considered as the natural infirmity of the Constitution. He was not prepared to abolish them. The limb was mortified, but amputation might be death [the orator forgot that to leave the mortified limb would be equally death]. His plan was to increase the county representation, which was still pure and uncorrupted. He urged the increase of another member to each county, both in England and in Scotland. He thought that increase would be " the only security against the profligacy of the times, the corruption of the people, and the ambition of the Crown." How utterly inadequate this reform would prove, in the immense preponderance over counties and large towns of the rotten boroughs, we know now. But it was sixty years before the nation succeeded in carrying any reform at all.

Over and over again Chatham perorated in the Peers about the discontents in the nation, the irritation produced by the conduct of the ministers of the Crown, and of the " influence behind the Crown," in which he insisted on believing. His doctrine was that manifest discontent in the nation was sufficient ground for urgent action, that the Peers were the hereditary advisers of the Crown, that it was a pressing crisis which called them to be united, and to make their common counsel reach the throne, in spite of the efforts of the open and the concealed evil counsellors at Court.

"It was the duty of that House to inquire into the causes

of that notorious dissatisfaction expressed by the whole English nation, to state these causes to their Sovereign, and then to give him their best advice in what manner he ought to act. The privileges of the House of Peers, however transcendent, however appropriated to them, stood, in fact, upon the broad bottom of the people."

". . . Let us be cautious how we admit an idea that our rights stand on a footing different from those of the people. Let us be cautious how *we invade the liberties of our fellow-subjects, however near, however remote: for be assured, my Lords, that in whatever part of the Empire you suffer slavery to be established, whether it be in America, or in Ireland, or here at home, you will find it a disease which spreads by contact, and soon reaches from the extremities to the heart.* The man who has lost his own freedom becomes from that moment an instrument in the hands of an ambitious prince, to destroy the freedom of others. The liberty of the subject is invaded not only in provinces, but here at home. The English people are loud in their complaints, they complain with one voice the injuries they have received; they demand redress, and depend upon it, my Lords, that one way or other they will have redress. They will never return to a state of tranquillity until they are redressed; nor ought they; for in my judgment, my Lords, and I speak it boldly, it were better for them to perish in a glorious contention for their rights, than to purchase a slavish tranquillity at the expense of a single iota of the Constitution."

How radically different was all this, both in substance and in form, from the language of Walpole, or of Burke, or even of Charles Fox. It was the language of Pym, of Somers, of Russell, of Brougham, and of Bright. It was in this that Chatham was the precursor of the advanced reformers of the nineteenth century, as he was the heir of the revolutionist leaders of the seventeenth century. Chatham was a real, and not a pinchbeck, Imperialist, as he was, I think, the first to use habitually the term *Empire* in its true sense. To him all men within the dominions of the Crown, of whatever colour and under whatever sun, were subjects of the King, and equally entitled to freedom. To him oppression, injustice, and violation of law, wherever done, were wrongs done to the nation as a whole, outrages which put their own liberties in peril. To him good government and justice were paramount needs for every citizen, whether they were threatened in Ireland, in Scotland, in England, in America, or in India. Chatham never countenanced the view that "Empire" meant small colonies of white settlers, holding in serfdom vast masses of some inferior race.

It was this conception of the solidarity of interests, as we might now say, which caused him to fling himself with such energy and with such persistence into the miserable series of squabbles about Wilkes and the Middlesex election. Chatham loathed and despised Wilkes as a man and as an agitator, and he always haughtily refused to interfere in any election. But in the matter of Wilkes being incapacitated for election by resolution of one House—the Commons declaring elected a candidate whom the electors had rejected—Chatham saw an illegal and unconstitutional attack on the rights of every elector in the kingdom. And on behalf of the principle of free representation of the people, he vehemently and persistently repudiated the action of the servile House of Commons under the influence of an arrogant King and his creatures. There can be no use in going into the details of the trumpery Middlesex election debates. Chatham from first to last upheld common sense, law, and wise policy. His view of the constitutional questions was entirely sound, was soon afterwards accepted by both parties, and is now settled law. In maintaining it, he confronted and overwhelmed not only the feeble spokesmen of the Court and the Government, sundry able and irresolute peers, but the weighty learning of Lord Mansfield himself. Mansfield was undoubtedly one of the most consummate lawyers in our history, as well as one of the subtlest and most persuasive logicians. But he was a coward, given to intrigue, always the advocate, and never the statesman. When Chatham denounced the act of the Commons in attempting to incapacitate Wilkes from being elected, and moved an amendment in the Lords to declare that they thereby "deprived the electors of Middlesex of their free choice of a representative," Mansfield made a powerful reply. From the point of view of strict constitutional law, Mansfield was right; and his speech is a classical exposition of the doctrine. He spoke as a judge rather than a peer. He insisted that the House of Commons had done illegal things in the matter of general warrants, which the judges could and did redress. In the matter of expelling Wilkes, in rejecting Wilkes's re-election to Middlesex, whether they had acted with wisdom, or indiscretion—and on this he, Mansfield, would never express what he thought as a peer—there was no court of law which could decide the question; much less could the House of Lords decide it. Both Houses were the sole courts of justice for their own rules and resolutions. Right or wrong, it was not for the other House to correct them.

In all this, Mansfield spoke as the great lawyer he

was. It was no doubt irregular, and perhaps impolitic at the moment, for Chatham to raise a formal amendment with Wilkes's name in it, and to force a division in the Lords. Mansfield and the large majority of the House were technically right in refusing to bring their own House of Peers into direct collision with the House of Commons. But it would be pedantic to regret that Chatham should have used the opportunity of his seat among the Peers to express in noble and passionate words the folly, the lawlessness, and the servility of the Commons in truckling to the Court. And in the Commons itself Lord Granby, Sir George Savile, and Burke, used the same language as Chatham and Camden, the Lord Chancellor, had used in the Lords. Walpole once wrote : " When Lord Mansfield was silent, as his fears now made him, Chatham was far superior to all his other adversaries ; *they were babies to him.*"

In this debate of 3rd January 1770, Chatham promised his hearty co-operation with Lord Rockingham. Whatever there had been in the past, " cordial union," he said, was now " indissoluble "—not in order to share the sweets of office, but to save the State. Would that it could have been maintained ! Lord Rockingham and his friends were honest, just, sensible men, guided by one man of splendid genius. Rockingham himself was over-cautious, inarticulate, proud, reserved, and commonplace. Shelburne, the ablest of Chatham's friends, was deeply distrusted as self-interested, disloyal, and insincere. Burke, with all his genius, was, and felt himself to be, a follower, not a leader ; he was satirical, touchy, jealous ; too subtle and doctrinaire for a great statesman. Chatham was an effervescent man of action, magnanimous and profoundly clear-visioned, but fiercely impatient of the moderation and niceties of the theorists. In the result Chatham, Rockingham, Shelburne, and Burke, sought the same ends in somewhat similar ways; but they failed to form an "indissoluble union," and too often suspected and thwarted each other.

Time after time Chatham returned to the struggle over the Middlesex election. He supported George Grenville's Bill for trying controverted elections. In May 1770, he brought in a Bill "for reversing the adjudications of the House of Commons" in the case of Wilkes and Colonel Luttrell. It is obvious that such a Bill, suggested to him by Lord Mansfield, perhaps in derision, was *brutum fulmen*, except as it enabled Chatham to make a great speech. And a great and fierce speech he made. "A corrupt House of Commons invert all law and order." "A majority in that House becomes a minister's state-engine, to effect the worst of purposes, and to produce such monstrous and unconstitutional acts, one cannot help exclaiming in the language of Shakespeare—

> 'Fie on it ! Oh fie !
> 'Tis an unweeded garden, things
> Rank and gross in nature possess it merely.'"

He hoped his Majesty would soon open his eyes. "He esteemed the King in his personal capacity, and he revered him in his political one." Four days afterwards, he moved again that the advice given to his Majesty (when he answered the address of the City of

London) was "of a most dangerous tendency." Ten days later he moved an address to the Throne to dissolve Parliament. As might have been foreseen, all of these motions were negatived by large majorities.

"Purity of Parliament is the corner-stone in the commonwealth"; to secure it was needed "a more full and equal representation," was the keynote of Chatham's reply to the City of London's address, as it was of his own conduct in Parliament. Again, in November in the same year, 1770, he returned to the Middlesex election in a fresh attack on Lord Mansfield, whose direction to the Jury in the famous libel case of printing Junius's 35th Letter, *To the King*, Chatham challenged. Mansfield's ruling was upheld by the judges, but met with violent criticism and public indignation until the point was settled by Fox's Libel Act in 1792, which declared that juries were entitled to bring in a general verdict of "guilty" or "not guilty" upon the whole question submitted to them. Thus after twenty-two years this famous controversy was settled by legislation, in the sense which Chatham had vainly struggled to maintain against the lawyers of his age.

Again he called for a dissolution, an appeal to the nation to decide the right, if one branch of the legislature could usurp the power to invade the liberty of the subject. The House of Commons, he said, had become odious to the present age, and their memory would be detested by posterity. He inveighed against the practice of modern judges to reserve to the bench the exclusive right to decide what constituted a *libel*. "The matter of libel—of public libel—was generally a *political* matter; and the question, whether a paper was a libel or not, was not a question of *law*, but a question of *politics*, in which ministers indulged their passion of revenge, and the courts of law became their instruments of gratification." Mansfield made a feeble and dilatory plea, in effect declined to reply. And in December, Chatham followed up the attack with even greater personal bitterness.

He now challenged the course taken by Lord Mansfield in the trial, boldly affirming that in his decision he had gone out of his legal limits, and had *travelled out of the record*, by introducing statements which he volunteered to give, but which were not properly in evidence. Chatham declared that "the conduct of the noble judge was irregular, extrajudicial, and unprecedented"—nay more, that his real motive for doing what he knew to be wrong was to take the opportunity of telling the public *extrajudicially* that three other judges agreed with him in the doctrine he had laid down. Whether Lord Mansfield could have successfully repelled this fierce attack, he made no attempt to do so, and Chatham's friends and Junius asserted that he was cowed and conscious of wrong. A furious pamphlet duel was waged between *Nerva* for Mansfield and *Phalaris* for Chatham.

In the following year, when the foolish government of Lord North, with his servile majority in the House of Commons, were dragged into their futile struggle with the printers of their debates, and then with the City of London; and had committed to the Tower the Lord Mayor, Brass Crosby, and Alderman Oliver, on the question of privilege, Chatham again returned to the charge. The report of his speech runs thus :—

"He entered largely into the consideration of the state of the country ; the depraved system of government, which had, in a very few years, reduced us from a most flourishing to a most miserable condition. He went through the whole proceedings of the House of Commons in the late business of the Printers, and arraigned every part of it in the strongest terms. He warmly defended the City magistrates in the conscientious discharge of their duty ; for the House, in committing them to prison without hearing their defence on the question of privilege, had been guilty of a gross and palpable act of tyranny ; that they had heard the prostituted electors of Shoreham in defence of an agreement to sell a borough by auction, and had refused to hear the Lord Mayor of London in defence of the laws of England ; that their expunging, by force, the entry of a recognizance, was the act of a *mob*, not of a Parliament ; that their daring to assume a power of stopping all prosecutions by their vote struck at once at the whole system of the laws ; that it was solely to the measures of the government, equally violent and absurd, that Mr. Wilkes owed all his importance ; that the King's ministers, supported by the slavish concurrence of the House of Commons, had made him a person of the greatest consequence in the kingdom ; that they had made him an Alderman of the City of London, and representative of the County of Middlesex ; and now they will make him Sheriff, and in due course, Lord Mayor of London ; that the proceedings of the House of Commons in regard to this gentleman made the very name of Parliament ridiculous." "To save the institution from contempt, this House must be dissolved. To resist the enormous influence of the Crown, some stronger barriers must be erected." And he now declared himself *a convert to triennial Parliaments*—which till now he had opposed. In May 1771, he moved an address to the King to dissolve Parliament "to compose" this alarming warfare, which may endanger the Constitution and tend to shake the tranquillity of the kingdom.

This motion, like all the others, was promptly negatived, and came to nothing. But every word he

had uttered was true. Every principle he affirmed has
been accepted and is now the law and practice of the
Constitution. Chatham in this, as in so many things,
was two or three generations before his age. His
forecasts were somewhat premature, however just and
wise. He told Lord Buchan—"before the end of this
century, either the Parliament will reform itself from
within, or be reformed with a vengeance from without." It would be an error to belittle the importance
of this famous brawl, owing to the vile character of
Wilkes or the ineptitude of the King and his creatures.
It was really the birth of the freedom of the Press and
the influence of political criticism on the conduct of
government.

At every point Chatham strove to resist the growing
prerogative of the Crown and the increasing degradation of the Commons. As to the "Nabobs" he cried
out—"the riches of Asia have been poured in upon
us, and have brought with them not only Asiatic
luxury, but Asiatic principles of government. Without connections, without any natural interest in the
soil, the importers of foreign gold have forced their
way into Parliament, by such a torrent of private
corruption, as no private hereditary fortune can
resist." He persisted in affirming the secret influence
of Lord Bute, though the quondam Favourite was
then abroad. And when the Duke of Grafton told
him that these suspicions were "the effects of a distempered mind brooding over its own discontents,"
he angrily retorted that his disease had never incapacitated him so as to forsake his principles. This
was no doubt true: the quarrel was a melancholy

outburst on both sides. Chatham, nominally First
Minister, found, on recovering his health, that the
ministry under the feeble or indolent leading of
Grafton, had allowed all the measures decided on
before his retirement to be not only neglected but
reversed. Chatham in his wrath suspected that
Grafton had been in collusion with Bute. The truth
was this. Bute had nothing to do with it. Grafton
was not in collusion with any one; but he was unstable, easy, and inert. The only secret influence was
that of George himself, whose grasping and dogged
nature made him the evil genius of his age.

On the civil list debate Chatham inveighed against
any attempt to conceal the expenditure from Parliament. The late good old King, he said, was sincere,
and allowed you to know "whether he liked you or
disliked you." Now, George III., it must be allowed,
was elaborately gracious to Chatham in person, but
at heart was his bitter enemy. "I will trust no
Sovereign in the world," said Chatham, "with the
means of purchasing the liberties of the people. Does
he mean, by drawing the purse-strings of his subjects,
to spread corruption through the people, to procure
a Parliament, like a packed jury, ready to acquit his
ministers at all adventures." Chatham was certainly
sincere enough outside the royal closet, and allowed
King or subject to know "whether he trusted you or
distrusted you"! Never did he speak truer word
than when he wrote that "he was resolved to be in
earnest for the public, and should be *a scarecrow of
violence* to the gentle warblers of the grove, the
moderate Whigs and temperate statesmen."

Rockingham and his friends were honest and honourable men—so were they all, all honourable men—but "that *moderation, moderation!* was the burden of the song among the body." That was the root difference between Chatham and the Rockingham connection. Rockingham was at best a very "moderate Whig." Burke for the present was also a moderate Whig, though in his heart of hearts a passionate Tory, and in his inmost brain ever a keen Conservative. Chatham was a passionate Whig of the "Glorious Revolution": constantly breaking out to be "a scarecrow of violence," by design rather than intemperance. It is this which explains the incompatibility that ever kept Chatham and Burke asunder. Burke's grand essay in 1770, *Thoughts on the Present Discontents*, with all its wisdom and eloquence, was a partisan defence of the feeble and commonplace rule of Rockingham, and an oblique censure on Chatham and his friends, who were endeavouring to form a united party. Chatham was quite right when he wrote to Rockingham that the essay had done harm to the cause. And Burke was quite wrong—ignobly and petulantly wrong—when, twenty years afterwards, he called this "a knavish letter." It was a temperate and sensible reply to a criticism which was ill-timed as well as unjust. It was unworthy of Burke to justify the well-meaning Rockingham at the expense of the high-souled Chatham.

Though the state of Parliament and the Constitution mainly absorbed Chatham's energy on his return to public life, he entered with keenness into the questions of foreign policy. France had purchased from Genoa the island of Corsica during Chatham's retirement. In his speech in 1770 he expressed his regret in these words :—" France has obtained a more useful and important acquisition in one *pacific* campaign, than in any of her *belligerent* campaigns. It is too much the temper of this country to be insensible of the approach of danger, until it comes upon us with accumulated terror." Nor is it too fanciful to speculate that if Chatham had retained his power and his health for but another year, Napoleon would not have been a Frenchman, for Chatham never would have suffered Corsica to pass to France.

But a far more stirring incident roused him two years afterwards in the affair of the seizure by Spain of the Falkland Islands. Peace was unbroken, and ministers and the nation suspected no attack, when Chatham, in urging an increase in the number of seamen, broke forth in a prophetic outburst :—"I pledge myself that, at this very hour, a *blow of hostility* has been struck against us by our old inveterate enemies in some quarter of the world." He had in truth divined that the efforts made by Choiseul in France, and by Grimaldi in Spain, to restore their navies, and to overthrow the maritime ascendency of Britain, were about to result in some overt act. Some months after-wards the country was roused to fury by the news that a Spanish armament had seized the Falkland Islands, lying one hundred leagues east of the Straits of Magellan, and had expelled a weak British force then in possession. These distant islands had been alternately claimed and occupied by Spaniards, French, and British. But the forcible ejection of a British governor, with his small military and naval detachment, was more than the

English people could endure. War with Spain was thought to be inevitable. All eyes turned to Chatham. The crisis roused him to all his old fire. The nation hung upon his words; and he poured forth one of his most masterly orations on the international relations and the maritime problems of the Empire.

We may at this time ignore the violence with which Chatham stormed against the ignorance, neglect, and treachery of the ministers who had reduced the country to a condition as deplorable at home as it was despicable abroad. Nor can we take seriously his denunciations of the meanness and craftiness of the Spaniards, the cunning of their merchants and their officers, and even the bad faith of the King of Spain, who disowned the thief, and profits by the theft, as a common "receiver of stolen goods." He then broke forth into the famous appeal :—

"Let us have peace, my Lords, but let it be honourable, let it be secure. A patched-up peace will not do—by which a war may be deferred, but cannot be avoided. . . . I know the strength and preparation of the House of Bourbon; I know the defenceless, unprepared condition of this country. . . . I will tell these young ministers the true source of intelligence. It is sagacity. Sagacity to compare causes and effects; to judge the present state of things, and discern the future, by a careful review of the past. Oliver Cromwell, who astonished mankind by his intelligence, did not derive it from spies in every cabinet in Europe; he drew it from the cabinet of his own sagacious mind. He observed facts and traced them forward to their consequences. From what was, he concluded what must be, and he never was deceived. . . . In the late war we had 85,000 seamen employed. We now have but 16,000, and it is now proposed to raise this to 25,000. But the forty ships of the line, now to be commissioned, with their frigates, will require 40,000 seamen. . . . Permit me now to

state the extent and variety of the service to be provided."
"The first great and acknowledged object of national defence,
in this country, is to maintain such a superior naval force at
home, that even the united fleets of France and Spain may
never be masters of the Channel. If that should ever happen,
what is there to hinder their landing in Ireland, or even upon
our own coasts? . . . The second naval object with an English
minister should be to maintain at all times a powerful Western
squadron. In the profoundest peace it should be respectable;
in war it should be formidable. Without it, the colonies, the
commerce, the navigation of Great Britain, lie at the mercy of
the House of Bourbon.

"The third object indispensable is to maintain such a force in
the Bay of Gibraltar as may be sufficient to cover that garrison,
to watch the motions of the Spaniards, and to keep open the
communication with Minorca. At this hour, he said, there
were but eleven ships ready equipped for the defence of the
Channel, one ship at Jamaica, one at the Leeward Islands,
and one at Gibraltar; and if these places were attacked, they
must fall." "When the defence of Great Britain or Ireland is
in question, it is no longer a point of honour; it is not the
security of foreign commerce, or foreign possessions; we are
to contend for the very being of the state." "If the House of
Bourbon make a wise and vigorous use of the actual advantages
they have over us, it is more than probable that on this day
month we may not be a nation." "When I compare the
numbers of our people, estimated highly at seven millions,
with the population of France and Spain, usually computed
at twenty-five millions, I see a clear self-evident impossibility
for this country to contend with the united power of the
House of Bourbon, merely upon the strength of its own
resources. They who talk of confining a great war to naval
operations only, speak without knowledge or experience. We
can no more command the disposition than the events of a
war. Wherever we are attacked, there we must defend."

· · ·

He then turned to defend the alliance with Frederick
of Prussia—"that wonderful man whose talents do
honour to human nature." Alliances with German

princes might be not only useful, but necessary. But
before all things we had to look to the internal condition of this country. We might look abroad for
wealth, or triumphs, or luxury; but England is the
main stay, the last resort of the whole Empire.
"Could it be expected that Englishmen would unite
heartily in defence of a government by which they
feel themselves insulted and oppressed? Restore them
to their rights; that was the way to make them
unanimous. It is not a ceremonious recommendation
from the Throne, that can bring back peace and harmony
to a discontented people. That insipid annual opiate
has been administered so long that it has lost its effect.
Something substantial, something effectual must be
done."

He closed with a furious invective against the men
in the City of London "who live in riot and luxury
upon the plunder of the ignorant, the innocent, the
helpless—the miserable jobbers of 'Change Alley, or
the lofty Asiatic plunderers of Leadenhall Street—the
monied interest, that blood-sucker, that muck-worm,
which calls itself the friend of government—that
advances money to government, and takes special
care of its own emoluments—the whole race of com-
missaries, jobbers, contractors clothiers, and remitters
—not the honest industrious tradesman or the fair
merchant—who are the prime source of national wealth."
He protested that he could never again be a minister:
that a strong ministry was needed: it must be popular
—not founded on any family connection. Those now
in office were balancing between a war that they
ought to have foreseen, and for which they had made

no provision, and an ignominious compromise. He warned them of their danger. If they were forced into war they stand at the hazard of their heads. If they made an ignominious compromise, let them consider if they would be able to walk the streets in safety.

Louis XV. shrank from war. Spain gave way, and restored the islands. It was soon afterwards abandoned, and has been recovered within recent years. It was said at the time that "Chatham's very name would prevent war." Perhaps his speech did. This speech of Chatham's was the occasion of Dr. Johnson's famous reply that it was "the feudal gabble of a man who is every day lessening that splendour of character which once illuminated the kingdom, then dazzled, and afterwards influenced it." An apt summary of the hostile view of Chatham's career.

CHAPTER XII

DEFENCE OF AMERICA

At last a man arose whose deeds spoke for him, the frag-
ments of whose eloquence were passed far and wide from
mouth to ear, and did not lose the stamp of their quality in
the carrying. With his broad heart, his swift perception,
and his capacious intellect, Chatham knew America, and he
loved her ; and he was known and loved by her in return.
He had done more for her than any ruler had done for any
country since William the Silent saved and made Holland; and
she repaid him with a true loyalty. When the evil day came,
it was to Chatham that she looked for the good offices which
might avert an appeal to arms. When hostilities had broken
out, she fixed on him her hopes of an honourable peace. And
when he died—in the very act of confessing her wrongs, though
of repudiating and condemning the establishment of that
national independence on which her own mind was by that
time irrevocably set—she refused to allow that she had any-
thing to forgive him, and mourned for him as a father of her
people.

IN these words the latest historian of the *American
Revolution*—Sir George Trevelyan, himself both statesman and historian, one of a family of statesmen and
historians—sums up the last years of Chatham's career.
These years were in many ways the grandest of his
life. He stood alone without a party or a group behind him. He was continually disabled by disease, and
forced to withdraw for long periods together. He had
against him prejudice and apathy in the ruling class;

overwhelming majorities in Parliament; insolent, blind, unscrupulous ministers; an arrogant bigot on the throne. Against such opposition he could not change, he could scarcely affect, the course of events. But in public and in private he poured out his indignation, his appeals to reason and to justice, his despair. He touched the hearts and brains of all the finer spirits of the age; he roused a generous sympathy in the American people; and he did much to mitigate the bitterness which they not unnaturally felt, and long have continued to nourish, against the nation of their oppressors.

When George Grenville proposed his Stamp Act of 1765, Chatham was ill in bed, and remained for that year absent from Parliament. When the Stamp Act was repealed in the following year it had been mainly by the indignant appeal of Chatham, who "*rejoiced that America had resisted.*" When Townshend in 1768 carried his fatal law to tax colonial imports, Chatham was not only prostrate and absent, but unable to know what was being passed. His just indignation broke forth in public and in private, when he returned to political action, and found the irreparable mischief which had been done under cover of his own name.

"America sits heavy upon my mind," he wrote to Lord Shelburne. Again he wrote on the Boston Tea outrage: "I am extremely anxious about the measures now depending, with regard to America, and I consider the fate of Old England as being at stake, not less than that of the New." He thought compensation should, and would, be offered for the violent destruction of the East India Company's tea cargo. "Perhaps a fatal desire to take advantage of this guilty tumult of the Bostonians, in order to crush the spirit of liberty among the Americans in general, has taken possession of the heart of the government. If that mad and cruel measure should be pushed, one need not be a prophet to say, England has seen her best days." "America disfranchised, and her charter mutilated, may, I forebode, resist; and the cause become general on that vast continent. If this happen, England is no more, how big words soever the sovereign in his parliament of Great Britain may utter."

He wrote to the Sheriff of London in 1774: "What infatuation and cruelty to accelerate the sad moment of war! Every step on the side of government, in America, seems calculated to drive the Americans into open resistance, vainly hoping to crush the spirit of liberty, in that vast continent, at one successful blow; but millions must perish there before the seeds of freedom will cease to grow and spread in so favourable a soil; and in the meantime devoted England must sink herself, under the ruins of her own foolish and inhuman system of destruction." "Maryland cannot wear chains! Would to Heaven it were equally plain that the oppressor, England, is not doomed, one day, to bind them round her own hands, and wear them patiently!" He rejoices in "the manly wisdom and calm resolution" of the Declaration of Rights by the American Congress, and will not believe that "freemen in England can wish to see three millions of Englishmen slaves in America."

To Chatham from first to last this was a Civil War,

of peculiar peril and injustice. He clearly divined
the issue. He did not overrate the infatuation of the
Court party, nor the indomitable forces they were
about to engage. He no doubt did estimate too
strongly the dangers to English liberty and the
ruinous consequences to our country of the inevitable
defeat. The condition of Britain after the surrender
of York Town was indeed humiliating. But the fore-
bodings of Chatham as to the decline of his country
and the establishment of a despotism at home were
hardly verified. Lecky, Trevelyan, and our recent
historians have all drawn attention to the fears of the
Whig Leaders, that the expulsion of the King's forces
from the United States would mean the decadence of
our country and the ruin of the Constitution. But
Chatham's conviction of the wrong and the danger
of the war was shared to the full by Burke and by
Rockingham, by Charles Fox, by Lord Shelburne, and
the Duke of Richmond.

It was not till May 1774 that Chatham again
appeared in Parliament. Disaffection and riot in
New England was now breaking out into war. He
made an impassioned protest against any taxation
of the Colonists, and against the methods of military
coercion by which the taxation was being enforced.
He called "Taxation, that father of American
Sedition."

"My Lords, I am an old man, and would advise the noble
Lords in office to adopt a more gentle mode of governing
America; for the day is not far distant, when America may
vie with these Kingdoms, not only in arms, but in arts also."
"This has always been my received and unalterable opinion,
and I will carry it to my grave, that *this country has no right*

under Heaven to tax America. It is contrary to all the principles of justice and civil policy, which neither the exigencies of the State, nor even an acquiescence in the taxes, could justify upon any occasion whatever."

In 1775 Chatham entered into close relations with Benjamin Franklin, the delegate from the American Colonies; and he publicly introduced him to the House of Lords, when he himself moved an address to the King to withdraw the troops from Boston. He stoutly maintained the right, the duty of the people of America, to resist. He derided the feeble means by which coercion was attempted to be enforced. With all his warmest love for the British troops, he said, their situation was truly unworthy; penned up, pining in inglorious inactivity. They were an army of impotence—an army of impotence and contempt; but to make the folly equal to the disgrace, they were an army of irritation and vexation. All attempts to impose servitude on such men, to establish despotism over such a mighty continental *nation*, must be vain, must be fatal. "We shall be *forced ultimately to retreat*; let us retreat while we can, not when we must. We must necessarily undo these violent oppressive acts : they must be repealed—you will repeal them; I pledge myself for it, that you will in the end repeal them; I stake my reputation on it : I will consent to be taken for an idiot, if they are not finally repealed. Avoid, then, this humiliating disgraceful necessity." Every motive of justice and of policy, of dignity and of prudence, he continued, urged them to allay the ferment in America by withdrawing the troops from Boston, by repealing the Acts. Every danger and every hazard impended to deter them from perseverance in their ruinous measures, foreign war hanging over their heads by a slight and brittle thread—France and Spain watching their conduct and waiting for the maturity of their errors.

He followed this up by a complicated Declaratory Bill, which he prepared in conference with Franklin, but which it is needless to set forth in detail. It would not have sufficed to content the Americans, and it was perhaps designed as a subject for discussion rather than legislation. It was summarily rejected by the Lords, though the Duke of Cumberland voted in the minority of thirty-two. On 4th July 1776 the Congress issued the *Declaration of Independence*, which caused renewed excitement in England, and a revulsion of popular feeling to continue the war. Chatham was not carried away by this shock, but he was unable to speak in public. During the whole of the year 1776 he was retained in the country by disease. It was not until May 1777 that he again appeared in Parliament. He came wrapped in flannels, and supported upon crutches. He said :—

"The gathering storm might break ; it has already opened and in part burst. If an end be not put to this war, there is an end to this country. America has carried us through four wars, and will now carry us to our death, if things were not taken in time. You may ravage—you cannot conquer ; it is impossible : you cannot conquer the Americans. I might as well talk of driving them before me with this crutch !"

In October 1777 General Burgoyne surrendered his whole army prisoners of war. Before the news reached this country, Chatham made another impassioned appeal against measures which had reduced this late flourishing Empire to ruin and contempt.

"Not only the power and strength of the country are wasting away and expiring; but her well-earned glories, her true honour, her substantial dignity, are sacrificed. France has insulted you; she has encouraged and sustained America; and whether America be wrong or right, the dignity of this country ought to spurn the officious insult of French interference. As to conquest, it is impossible. You may swell every expense, and every effort, still more extravagantly; pile and accumulate every assistance you can buy or borrow; traffic and barter with every pitiful little German prince, that sells and sends his subjects to the shambles of a foreign prince; your efforts are for ever vain and impotent—doubly so for this mercenary aid on which you rely; for it irritates, to an incurable resentment, the minds of your enemies, to overrun them with the mercenary sons of rapine and plunder; devoting them and their possessions to the rapacity of hireling cruelty! If I were an American, as I am an Englishman, while a foreign troop was landed in my country, I never would lay down my arms—never—never—never! Your own army is infected with the contagion of these illiberal allies. The spirit of plunder and of rapine is gone forth among them. Who is the man that has dared to authorise as associate to our armies the tomahawk and scalping-knife of the savage? To call into civilised alliance the wild and inhuman savage of the woods; to delegate to the merciless Indian the defence of disputed rights, and to wage the horrors of his barbarous war against our brethren? These enormities cry aloud for redress and punishment: unless thoroughly done away, it will be a stain on the national character—it is a violation of the Constitution—I believe it is against law. It is not the least of our national misfortunes, that the strength and character of our army are thus impaired: infected with the mercenary spirit of robbery and rapine—familiarised to the horrid scenes of savage cruelty, it can no longer boast of the noble and generous principles which dignify a soldier; no longer sympathise with the dignity of the royal banner, nor feel the pride, pomp, and circumstance of glorious war, that make 'ambition virtue'! What makes ambition virtue?—the sense of honour. But is the sense of honour consistent with the spirit of plunder, or the practice of murder? Can it flow from mercenary motives, or can it prompt to cruel deeds? Besides these murderers and plunderers, let me ask our ministers —what other allies have they acquired? What other powers have they associated with their cause? Have they entered into alliance with the *King of the Gypsies*? Nothing is too low or too ludicrous to be consistent with their counsels."

Lord Suffolk rose and defended the employment of Indians, that it was justifiable to use "all the means that God and Nature put into our hands." This roused Chatham to the famous retort. He could not repress his indignation :—

"I know not what ideas that Lord may entertain of God and nature ; but I know that such abominable principles are equally abhorrent to religion and humanity. What ! to attribute the sacred sanction of God and nature to the massacres of the Indian scalping-knife—to the cannibal savage torturing, murdering, roasting, and eating—literally, *eating* the mangled victims of his barbarous battles !" . . . "These abominable principles, and this more abominable avowal of them, demand the most decisive indignation. I call upon that *Right Reverend* Bench, those holy ministers of the Gospel, and pious pastors of our Church ; I conjure them to join in the holy work, and vindicate the religion of their God : I appeal to the wisdom and the law of this *learned* Bench to defend and support the justice of their country : I call upon the Bishops to interpose the unsullied sanctity of their lawn,—upon the learned judges to interpose the purity of their ermine, to save us from this pollution :—I call upon the honour of your Lordships to reverence the dignity of your ancestors and to maintain your own : I call upon the spirit and humanity of my country to vindicate the national character :—I invoke the genius of the Constitution. From the tapestry that adorns these walls, the immortal ancestor of this noble Lord [Thomas Howard, first Earl of Suffolk] frowns with indignation at the disgrace of his

country.   In vain he led your victorious fleets against the
boasted Armada of Spain ; in vain he defended and established
the honour, the liberties, the religion, the Protestant religion
of this country against the arbitrary cruelties of Popery and
the Inquisition, if these more than popish cruelties and inquisi-
torial practices are let loose among us ; to turn forth into our
settlements, among our ancient connections, friends, and relations, the merciless cannibal, thirsting for the blood of man,
woman, and child—to send forth the infidel savage—against
whom ? against your Protestant brethren ; to lay waste their
country, to desolate their dwellings, and extirpate their race
and name, with these horrible hell-hounds of savage war ! " . . .
" I call upon your Lordships, and the united powers of the
State, to stamp on this awful subject an indelible stigma of the
public abhorrence.   I implore those holy prelates of our
religion to do away these iniquities from among us.   Let them
perform a lustration ; let them purify this House and this
country from this sin ; I am old and weak, and at present
unable to say more ; but my feelings and indignation were too
strong to have said less.   I could not have slept this night in
my bed, nor reposed my head on my pillow, without giving
this vent to my eternal abhorrence of such preposterous and
enormous principles."

A few weeks later Chatham supported the Duke of
Richmond's inquiry into the state of the nation, in
which he reviewed the perilous condition of the
country.   When the news of Burgoyne's surrender
came at the end of 1777, he defended the general and
his army, and justly declared them to have "been
sacrificed to the ignorance, temerity, and incapacity of
ministers."   He revived his protest against the use of
Indians—"a pollution of our national character ; a
stigma which all the waters of the Delaware and
Hudson would never wash away."   He challenged
the ministers to recall the mercenaries and to disband
the savages—to withdraw our troops entirely.   On

the motion for an adjournment of the House for six
weeks, he again spoke on 11th December 1777. He
insisted that the hereditary Council of the nation
should not take holiday when the nation was in
mourning. Nay more, it was in imminent peril—
"Safe no longer than its enemies think proper to
permit." He reviewed the state of our naval and
military defences, and exposed their weakness. "They
told you in the beginning, that 15,000 men would
traverse America, with scarcely the appearance of
interruption. Two campaigns have passed since they
gave us this assurance; treble that number has been
employed; and one of your armies, which composed
two-thirds of the force by which America was to be
subdued, has been totally destroyed, and is now led
captive through those provinces you call rebellious.
Those men whom you called cowards, poltroons,
runaways and knaves, are become victorious over your
veteran troops; and, in the midst of victory and the
flush of conquest, have set ministers an example of
moderation and magnanimity."

With the year 1778 the state of the nation was
darker than ever. The King and his ministers
doggedly persisted in the war. Troops could neither
be raised nor hired. France allied itself with the
Americans, and George declared war with France.
England had not a friend left. Her troops were
prisoners or blockaded in America. Her credit was
exhausted. Her fleet was unprepared; and she had
reason to fear attack from the united navies of France
and of Spain. In this terrible hour of peril there was
one man to whom all thoughts turned. Lord North,

who had long carried on this war against his own
conviction and had just declared the conquest of
America to be impossible, implored the King to accept
his own resignation and send for Chatham. Bute, the
quondam favourite, said Chatham was indispensable.
Mansfield, his inveterate enemy, said that without
him the ship would founder. Camden, Rockingham,
Burke, Richmond joined in the universal cry—Send
for Chatham.

Against all this George resisted with the dogged-
ness of a brute rather than of a monarch. He would
never see Chatham : he would lose his crown but
never would accept the Opposition. He would allow
North to call in Chatham as a subordinate, but the
cast and policy of the administration should not be
changed. Lecky calls this the most criminal act in
the whole reign of George III., as criminal as any act
of Charles I. Whatever the chances might have been,
it was too late. Chatham himself was at death's door.
The possibilities of any reconciliation or settlement
with America short of absolute separation were now at
an end. Even the magic of Chatham's name, and even
his genius at its zenith, now could have effected
nothing in the way of compromise. A French alliance
had bound the Americans to the common interest. A
French war had roused the national pride of Britons,
when it was seen that the Empire was about to be
broken up by the arms of their hereditary foe.

To this humiliation Chatham would not stoop. To
the American people, whom he loved and honoured,
he would concede everything. But to have America,
which he had rescued from France, again torn away

from us by the rival whom he had crushed—this
was a sacrifice to which he could not submit. His old
dread and jealousy of the House of Bourbon, which
had become almost a monomania with him, blazed up
with all its ancient fire. In this, the ardent patriot
extinguished in him the far-seeing statesman. We
can see to-day how far passion had misled him. Burke,
Rockingham, Fox, the Duke of Richmond—some of the
best brains of the Whig party—urged the immediate
recognition of American independence. Chatham died
in the act of protesting against it. And a cloud hung
over the sun of his renown as he sank to rest.

On the 7th of April 1778, the Duke of Richmond
moved an address to the Crown in the sense of their
group. Feeble as he was, in his seventieth year,
racked with pain, Chatham struggled at the hazard of
his life to attend and speak. He was led into the
House by his son William Pitt, the future statesman,
and his son-in-law, Lord Mahon. He was dressed in
black velvet, and covered to the knees in flannel.
Within his large wig little more of his countenace was
seen than his aquiline nose and his eye, which retained
its native fire. We are told, "He looked like a dying
man, yet never was seen a figure of more dignity : he
appeared like a being of a superior species." The
Lords stood up and made a lane for him to pass. He
bowed as he went on. Presently he rose slowly with
the aid of his crutches and the two young men. He
raised his head, and looking to Heaven he said—

"I thank God that I have been enabled to come here this
day to perform my duty. I am old and infirm—have one foot,
more than one foot in the grave—I have risen from my bed,

to stand up in the cause of my country—perhaps never again to speak in this House."

The stillness of the House was most touching. He continued to describe all the evils, the crimes, and the follies of the American war.

"My Lords," he broke forth, "I rejoice that the grave has not closed upon me; that I am still alive to lift up my voice against the dismemberment of this ancient and most noble monarchy! Shall this great kingdom now fall prostrate before the House of Bourbon? If we must fall, let us fall like men!"

The Duke of Richmond replied with cool sense to show the hopelessness of a war by Britain in her present forlorn state against the united forces of France, Spain, and America. He told the orator that even he would now find himself in impossible conditions. Chatham seemed roused and indignant. He struggled to his feet, and essayed to stand. Then he pressed his hand upon his heart and fell in convulsions. The peers near caught him in their arms. The House was cleared: he was carried to Downing Street, and shortly afterwards to his home at Hayes. On the 11th of May he died there in peace, surrounded by his wife and his children.

English Men of Letters

Edited by JOHN MORLEY

Popular Edition. Crown 8vo. Paper Covers, 1s.; Cloth, 1s. 6d. each
Library Edition. Crown 8vo. Gilt tops. Flat backs. 2s. net each

ADDISON. By W. J. COURTHOPE.

BACON. By Dean CHURCH.

BENTLEY. By Sir RICHARD JEBB.

BUNYAN. By J. A. FROUDE.

BURKE. By JOHN MORLEY.

BURNS. By Principal SHAIRP.

BYRON. By Professor NICHOL.

CARLYLE. By Professor NICHOL.

CHAUCER. By Dr. A. W. WARD.

COLERIDGE. By H. D. TRAILL.

COWPER. By GOLDWIN SMITH.

DEFOE. By W. MINTO.

DE QUINCEY. By Prof. MASSON.

DICKENS. By Dr. A. W. WARD.

DRYDEN. By Prof. SAINTSBURY.

FIELDING. By AUSTIN DOBSON.

GIBBON. By J. COTTER MORISON.

GOLDSMITH. By WILLIAM BLACK.

GRAY. By EDMUND GOSSE.

HAWTHORNE. By HENRY JAMES.

HUME. By Prof. HUXLEY, F.R.S.

JOHNSON. By Sir LESLIE STEPHEN, K.C.B.

KEATS. By SIDNEY COLVIN.

LAMB, Charles. By Canon AINGER.

LANDOR. By SIDNEY COLVIN.

LOCKE. By THOMAS FOWLER.

MACAULAY. By J. COTTER MORISON.

MILTON. By MARK PATTISON.

POPE. By Sir LESLIE STEPHEN, K.C.B.

SCOTT. By R. H. HUTTON.

SHELLEY. By J. A. SYMONDS.

SHERIDAN. By Mrs. OLIPHANT.

SIDNEY. By J. A. SYMONDS.

SOUTHEY. By Prof. DOWDEN.

SPENSER. By Dean CHURCH.

STERNE. By H. D. TRAILL.

SWIFT. By Sir LESLIE STEPHEN, K.C.B.

THACKERAY. By ANTHONY TROLLOPE.

WORDSWORTH. By F. W. H. MYERS.

NEW SERIES

Crown 8vo. Gilt tops. Flat backs. 2s. net each

Volumes Ready.

GEORGE ELIOT. By Sir LESLIE STEPHEN, K.C.B.

HAZLITT. By AUGUSTINE BIRRELL, K.C.

MATTHEW ARNOLD. By HERBERT W. PAUL.

RUSKIN. By FREDERIC HARRISON.

TENNYSON. By Sir ALFRED LYALL.

RICHARDSON. By AUSTIN DOBSON.

BROWNING. By G. K. CHESTERTON.

CRABBE. By the Rev. Canon AINGER.

FANNY BURNEY. By AUSTIN DOBSON.

JEREMY TAYLOR. By EDMUND GOSSE.

ROSSETTI. By A. C. BENSON.

MARIA EDGEWORTH. By the Hon. EMILY LAWLESS.

HOBBES. By Sir LESLIE STEPHEN, K.C.B.

ADAM SMITH. By FRANCIS W. HIRST.

SYDNEY SMITH. By GEORGE W. E. RUSSELL.

THOMAS MOORE. By STEPHEN GWYNN.

In Preparation.

EDWARD FITZGERALD. By A. C. BENSON.

ANDREW MARVELL. By AUGUSTINE BIRRELL, K.C.

MRS. GASKELL. By CLEMENT SHORTER.

CHARLES KINGSLEY. By G. K. CHESTERTON.

SHAKESPEARE. By Professor WALTER RALEIGH.

JAMES THOMSON. By G. C. MACAULAY.

SIR THOMAS BROWNE. By EDMUND GOSSE.

WALTER PATER. By A. C. BENSON.

MACMILLAN AND CO., LTD., LONDON

Twelve English Statesmen

Crown 8vo. 2s. 6d. each

. A Series of Short Biographies, not designed to be a complete roll of famous Statesmen, but to present in historic order the lives and work of those leading actors in our affairs who by their direct influence have left an abiding mark on the policy, the institutions, and the position of Great Britain among States.

WILLIAM THE CON-QUEROR. By EDWARD A. FREEMAN, D.C.L., LL.D., late Regius Professor of Modern History in the University of Oxford.

HENRY II.
By Mrs. J. R. GREEN.

EDWARD I.
By T. F. TOUT, M.A., Professor of History, The Owens College, Manchester.

HENRY VII.
By JAMES GAIRDNER.

CARDINAL WOLSEY.
By Bishop CREIGHTON, D.D., late Dixie Professor of Ecclesiastical History in the University of Cambridge.

ELIZABETH.
By E. S. BEESLY, M.A., Professor of Modern History, University College London.

OLIVER CROMWELL.
By FREDERIC HARRISON.

WILLIAM III.
By H. D. TRAILL.

WALPOLE.
By JOHN MORLEY.

CHATHAM.
By FREDERIC HARRISON.

PITT.
By Lord ROSEBERY.

PEEL.
By J. R. THURSFIELD, M.A., late Fellow of Jesus College, Oxford.

English Men of Action Series

Crown 8vo. Cloth. With Portraits. 2s. 6d. each

CAMPBELL (COLIN).
By ARCHIBALD FORBES.

CLIVE.
By Sir CHARLES WILSON.

COOK (Captain).
By Sir WALTER BESANT.

DAMPIER.
By W. CLARK RUSSELL.

DRAKE.
By JULIAN CORBETT.

DUNDONALD.
By the Hon. J. W. FORTESCUE.

GORDON (General).
By Sir W. BUTLER.

HASTINGS (Warren).
By Sir A. LYALL.

HAVELOCK (Sir Henry).
By A. FORBES.

HENRY V.
By the Rev. A. J. CHURCH.

LAWRENCE (Lord).
By Sir RICHARD TEMPLE.

LIVINGSTONE.
By THOMAS HUGHES.

MONK.
By JULIAN CORBETT.

MONTROSE.
By MOWBRAY MORRIS.

NAPIER (Sir Charles).
By Colonel Sir W. BUTLER.

NELSON.
By Prof. J. K. LAUGHTON.

PETERBOROUGH.
By W. STEBBING.

RALEIGH (Sir Walter)
By Sir RENNELL RODD.

RODNEY.
By DAVID HANNAY.

STRAFFORD.
By H. D. TRAILL.

WARWICK, the King-Maker
By C. W. OMAN.

WELLINGTON.
By GEORGE HOOPER.

WOLFE.
By A. G. BRADLEY.

MACMILLAN AND CO., LTD., LONDON

5.3.05